FOOLS OF TIME

THE ALEXANDER LECTURES

The Alexander Lectureship was founded in honour of Professor W. J. Alexander, who held the Chair of English at University College, University of Toronto, from 1889 to 1926. Each year the Lectureship brings to the University a distinguished scholar or critic to give a course of lectures on a subject related to English Literature.

NORTHROP FRYE

FOOLS

 OF

TIME

Studies in

Shakespearean

Tragedy

University of Toronto Press

DESIGNED BY ELLEN HUTCHISON

Preface and dedication

What follows is the original written version of the Alexander Lectures, delivered at Convocation Hall, University of Toronto, on March 15, 16, and 17, 1966. The oral version, considerably shorter and more concise, had its advantages, but for publication I felt that the longer form, with its greater number of examples and expanding passages, was preferable. This is the fifth series of lectures I have published, and two more series are in course of publication. But for all the experience I have had with it, I still find the public lecture a fantastically difficult genre, and nowhere more so than in a field so thoroughly worked over as Shakespearean tragedy. I can only hope that the constant effort to make the familiar statement into a fresh insight has here and there been successful.

I am greatly indebted to the Canada Council for a Fellowship that helped me to work on this and other projects.

The following preface was read at the beginning of the first lecture:

The invitation to deliver the Alexander Lectures came to me in England, when I had already contracted for two other series. Yet I accepted very promptly, and for two reasons. In the first place, I was deeply touched by the great and most unusual honour of being asked to contribute to this famous series on my own campus.

In the second place, the invitation came at almost the same moment as the news of the death of Professor A. S. P. Woodhouse. If it is not too pretentious to do so, I should like to dedicate these lectures to Professor Woodhouse's memory. Although I met him once or twice, I never really knew Professor Alexander, who retired from teaching in the year that I entered high school, but I did know of Professor Woodhouse's admiration for him, and it is mainly through Professor Woodhouse that I can attach myself personally to the teacher commemorated in this series.

I have only to add that the occasion of giving the lectures at the invitation of University College was made both pleasant and memorable by the kindness and hospitality of Professor Clifford Leech and Principal Douglas LePan of that College, and President Claude Bissell. The fact that all three are old friends did not diminish the sense of gracious welcome.

NORTHROP FRYE

Victoria College in the
University of Toronto
1967

Contents

My father as
he slept:
The tragedy
of order

My father as he slept: The tragedy of order

The basis of the tragic vision is being in time, the sense of the one-directional quality of life, where everything happens once and for all, where every act brings unavoidable and fateful consequences, and where all experience vanishes, not simply into the past, but into nothingness, annihilation. In the tragic vision death is, not an incident in life, not even the inevitable end of life, but the essential event that gives shape and form to life. Death is what defines the individual, and marks him off from the continuity of life that flows indefinitely between the past and the future. It gives to the individual life a parabola shape, rising from birth to maturity and sinking again, and this parabola movement of rise and fall is also the typical shape of tragedy. The mood of tragedy preserves our ambiguous and paradoxical feeling about death; it is inevitable and always happens, and yet, when it does happen, it carries with it some sense of the unnatural and premature. The naiveté of Marlowe's Tamburlaine, astonished by the fact that *he* should die when he has been wading through other men's blood for years, is an example, and even Shakespeare's Caesar, so thoroughly disciplined in his views of death in general, still finds his actual death a surprise.

Being in time is not the whole of the tragic vision: it is, in itself, the ironic vision. Because it is the basis of the tragic vision, the ironic and the tragic are often confused or identified. The nineteenth-century pessimism which produced the philosophy of Schopenhauer and the novels of Thomas Hardy seems to me ironic rather than tragic. So does the philosophy and literature of existentialism, which I think of, for reasons that may become clearer later on, as post-tragic. But tragedy, no less than irony, *is* existential: the conceptions that existential thinkers have tried to struggle with, care, dread, nausea, absurdity, authenticity, and the like, are all relevant to the theory of tragedy. Tragedy is also existential in a broader, and perhaps contradictory, sense, in that the experience of the tragic cannot be moralized or contained within any conceptual world-view. A tragic hero is a tragic hero whether he is a good or a bad man; a tragic action is a tragic action whether it seems to us admirable or villainous, inevitable or arbitrary. And while a religious or philosophical system that answers all questions and solves all problems may find a place for tragedy, and so make it a part of a larger and less tragic whole, it can never absorb the kind of experience that tragedy represents. That remains outside of all approaches to being through thought rather than existence. The remark of the dying Hotspur, "Thought's the slave of life," comes out of the heart of the tragic vision.

Tragedy revolves around the primary contract of man and nature, the contract fulfilled by man's death, death being, as we say, the debt he owes to nature. What makes tragedy tragic, and not simply ironic, is the presence in it of a counter-movement of being that we call the heroic, a capacity for action or passion, for doing or suffering, which is above ordinary human experience. This heroic energy, glorified by itself as something invincible which bursts the boundaries of normal experience, is the basis of romance. In tragedy the heroic is within the human context, and so is still limited and finite, formed and shaped by death. In Greek tragedy especially, we can see how death is both the punishment of the aggressor and the reward of his victim. This makes tragic sense, if not moral sense. But because the heroic is above the normal limits of experience, it also suggests something infinite imprisoned in the finite. This something infinite may be morally either good or bad, for the worst of men may still be a hero if he is big enough to anger or frighten the gods. Man may be infinite if he is infinite only in his evil desires. The hero is an individual, but being so great an individual he seems constantly on the point of being swept into titanic forces he cannot control. The fact that an infinite energy is driving towards death in tragedy means that the impetus of tragedy is *sacrificial*. Sacrifice expresses the principle that in human life the infinite takes the same direction as the finite.

Tragedy, then, shows us the impact of heroic energy on the human situation. The heroic is normally destroyed in the conflict, and the human situation goes on surviving. "A living dog is better than a dead lion," says the Preacher: whether better or not, the dialectic of tragedy works through to a situation in which the heroic is normally dead and the less heroic is all that can remain alive. Octavius and Aufidius may be shrewder and more prudent men than Mark Antony or Coriolanus, but they are smaller men. Tragedy often ends with the survivors forming, or about to form, a secondary or social contract, a relation among more ordinary men which

will achieve enough working justice or equity to minimize
further tragedy. In the worlds of Fortinbras and Malcolm
fewer ghosts will walk; after the deaths of Romeo and Juliet
there will be less lethal feuding in Verona.

Sometimes the social contract that forms at the end of a
tragedy is of great depth and significance, as it is in the
Oresteia; sometimes, in Greek tragedy, it exists only in the
final comments of the chorus; sometimes, as often in Shakespeare, it is merely an exhausted and demoralized huddle.
Whatever it is, it usually expresses some limiting or falling
away of perspective after the great heroic voices have been
silenced. This comes out clearly in the last two lines of
King Lear:

> The oldest hath borne most: we that are young
> Shall never see so much, nor live so long.

The basis of irony is the independence of the way things are
from the way we want them to be; in tragedy a heroic effort
against this independence is made and fails; we then come to
terms with irony by reducing our wants. In tragedy the ironic
vision survives the heroic one, but the heroic vision is the one
we remember, and the tragedy is for its sake. The more ironic
the tragedy, the fewer the central characters who die. In
Troilus and Cressida, though the setting is a battlefield where
men die like flies every day, none of the central characters
dies except the greatest of all, Hector; in *Timon of Athens*
nobody dies except the only noble character, Timon. Our
first tentative conclusion about the feelings roused in us by
the tragic experience, therefore, is something like this: the
heroic and the infinite have been; the human and finite are.

In Greek tragedy, the gods have the function of enforcing what we have called the primary contract of man and nature. The gods are to human society what the warrior aristocracy is to the workers within human society itself. Like aristocrats, they act toward their inferiors with a kind of rough justice, but they are by no means infallible, and we often glimpse their underlying panic about the danger that men will become too powerful. Man has certain duties toward the gods, and he expects, without having the right to claim, certain benefits in return. But as long as the gods are there, man is limited in his scope, ambitions, and powers. Men in Greek tragedy are *brotoi*, "dying ones," a word with a concrete force in it that our word "mortals" hardly conveys.

Such a view is by no means original with the Greeks: much earlier, for example, the Gilgamesh epic in Mesopotamia had portrayed the gods in a similar aristocratic role. There, the gods found that they could not continue to live without having to work: this being beneath their dignity, they created men to do the work for them. The epic then goes on to describe how man attempts and fails to achieve immortality. It is a very ironic story, but if we compare it with the Iliad we feel that the heroic, or distinctively tragic, component is missing. The intense interest that the gods in the Iliad take in the conflict going on below them is their response to the infinite quality in human heroism. They watch it, not with a detached ironic amusement, but with a tragic sense of engagement. For one thing, some of the heroes are their own progeny. The only moral check on their desire to seduce human women is the slave-owner's check, the fact that all children born of such a union will be lost in the lower society. We are occasionally reminded in the Iliad that the Olympian gods, no less than the Christian God, are losing their own sons in the human struggle, and, unlike the Christian God, they are compelled to leave their sons' souls in Hades.

As for the heroes themselves, their life sustains a continuous illusion. Nothing that is *done* in a heroic conflict has anything except death for its form, and the *klea andron* that Homer celebrates, the brave deeds of men, consist only in spilling and destroying life. In Sarpedon's speech to Glaucus in the Iliad there is one terrible instant of awareness in which Sarpedon says that if he could think of himself as ageless and immortal, like the gods, he would walk out of the battle at once. But, being a man, his life *is* death, and there is nowhere in life that is not a battlefield. Unlike his counterpart Arjuna in the *Bhagavadgita*, he can hope for no further illumination on that battlefield. The Greek heroes belong to a leisure class remote from our ordinary preoccupations; this gives them more time, not for enjoying life, but for doing what the unheroic cannot do: looking steadily and constantly into the abyss of death and nothingness. The Greek gods respect this, just as the Christian God respects the corresponding contemplative attitude, the *contemptus mundi*, on the part of the saint.

There are two kinds of death in Greek tragedy: ordinary death, which happens to everybody, and heroic death, which may be directly caused by the gods out of fear or anger, or, if not, has at any rate some peculiar significance, a marking out of a victim. Death may thus be seen as caused by the impersonal force of fate or by the will of the gods. Sometimes, as in the fall of Oedipus, an oracle or prophecy is being fulfilled, and this combines the two themes of divine will and natural event. Gods and fate both represent an order or balance in the scheme of things, the way things are. If this order is disturbed by human pride, boastfulness, or insatiable ambition, a personal divine force reacts to it, after which the pattern of ordinary fate reappears in human life. This reappearance is called nemesis. Death in itself is a natural event; a death brought about by the gods forcibly assimilates human life to nature. Thus the gods, however harsh in their wrath or jealousy, manifest by their actions a social and moral force in human life itself, the principle of stability, or living in the face of death, which in the soul is called temperance (*sophrosyne*) and in society justice.

The individual gods, like individual men, may be partial and passionate: Greek poets and philosophers, like their successors, could never quite solve the problem of how a being can be an individual and yet not ultimately finite. But even in Homer we can see how conflicts among the gods are contained within a single divine order, the will of Zeus. This single divine order corresponds to the order of temperance or stability among the conflicting impulses of the human mind. The Hippolytus of Euripides is a chaste and virtuous youth: in other words he is a worshipper of Artemis. He is eventually justified by his faith in Artemis, but he is so aggressively chaste and virtuous that he provokes the anger of Aphrodite and comes to grief. In relation to the whole group of Olympian gods, his chastity is excessive and unbalanced. But temperance and stability do not provide a static order; they are an ordering of powers and forces. Pentheus in *The Bacchae* tries to keep a tight grip on himself when confronted with

Dionysus, and is swept out of the way like a leaf in a hurricane.

In *The Birth of Tragedy* Nietzsche describes the Greek sense of the limited and finite as the "Apollonian" side of Greek culture. This is the sense that comes out particularly in the exquisite Greek feeling for plastic form, and which, in the verbal arts, ranges from the profoundest conceptions in Greek thought, Plato's *idea* and Aristotle's *telos*, to cautionary proverbs of the "nothing too much" type. The sense of infinite heroic energy Nietzsche identifies with the "Dionysian," where the individual is not defined and assigned a place in the scheme of things, but released by being dissolved into the drunken and frenzied group of worshippers. Nietzsche's Apollonian–Dionysian distinction is one of those central insights into critical theory that critics must sooner or later come to terms with, though coming to terms with it means, first of all, deciding whether the particular historical projection given to the insight is the best one. I use it because I find it illuminating for Shakespeare: I am quite prepared to believe that it may be less so for the Greeks, where Nietzsche's argument seems greatly weakened by what appears to me a preposterous view of Euripides. Nietzsche is on much sounder ground in saying that the spirit of tragedy was destroyed by a spirit he identifies with Socrates and associates with comedy and irony. Tragedy is existential: Socrates, with his conception of militant knowledge, begins an essentialist tradition in human thought. His disciple Plato is the greatest of all the essentialist philosophers, of those who have approached reality through thought rather than experience, and Plato's literary affinities are clearly with the comic poets, not the tragic ones.

We next meet tragedy in Seneca, whose tragedies are Greek subjects recollected in tranquillity. Or relative tranquillity: there are melodramatic qualities in Elizabethan drama that are popularly thought of as Senecan—ghosts screaming for revenge, an action full of horrors and with lots and lots of blood—but these are mainly generalizations from one Senecan play, *Thyestes*. In this play Atreus revenges himself on his brother by inviting him to dinner and serving him his children in a pie—an incident which reappears in *Titus Andronicus*— but even this is an authentic Greek theme. Seneca is, again, an essentialist philosopher, a Stoic, and for him the two contracts we have mentioned, the primary contract with gods and nature which is natural law, and the secondary social contract which is moral law, are identical. He tends to think of his characters as heroic in proportion to the extent to which they identify themselves with this law. They are heroic in endurance rather than in action, in their capacity to surmount suffering rather than in the power of their wills.

Hence rhetoric, the ability to express an articulate awareness of what is happening, has a function in Seneca that is quite different from its function in the three great Greeks. In the Greek plays the action is presented by the characters and represented by the chorus: the chorus has a role of response to the action that, like the music in an opera, puts the audience's emotion into focus. Seneca retains the chorus, but he has much less need for it: the rhetorical speeches take over most of the chorus's real dramatic functions. Even action, in Seneca, is constantly dominated by consciousness. To know is a higher destiny than to experience, and by virtue of his consciousness man may rank himself with the gods, in fact may even outgrow them. In Euripides' *Heracles* the hero's

feat of entering hell and carrying off Cerberus is a physical
feat so astounding that the goddess Here promptly sends
madness upon him. Otherwise, man will become too big for
his breeches. The important thing is not whether Heracles'
madness is internal or external in origin: the important thing
is that his madness is the kind of thing that inevitably happens
when the power of the gods is threatened. Seneca's Juno is
equally anxious to set limits to human power, but the madness
is, to a much greater extent, a weakness in Hercules himself
which she exploits. Seneca thinks of Hercules' feat as a
harrowing of hell, an allegory of the kind of power in man
that may eventually deliver him from the power of the gods,
unless, as Juno says, the gods can succeed in setting man to
war with himself. The source of the conflict, to use Greek
terms, is *praxis* in Euripides, a conflict in the dramatic action;
it is *theoria* in Seneca, a conflict of mental attitudes.

The early Elizabethan tragic dramatists, like Seneca,
developed a highly rhetorical texture, and had even less need
of a chorus. Again, gods are essential to the Greek conception
of tragedy, but they are not really essential to Senecan tragedy.
A later play in the Senecan tradition, *Octavia*, which intro-
duces the Emperor Nero and Seneca himself as characters,
has a ghost, but no gods, and indicates that if Roman tragedy
had survived it would have gone in the direction of historical
rather than mythical themes, the direction from which the
Elizabethans started. The Elizabethans had little place for the
gods either, which they regarded as personifications of natural
forces. This means that social and political situations have a
much more important place in Elizabethan than in Greek
tragedy. In Greek tragedy catastrophe is referred primarily to

the gods: crimes are offences against them, which is why purely ritual themes, such as leaving a body unburied, are so prominent. Royal figures are certainly important, but their subordination to the gods is always emphasized. Elizabethan tragedy not only had no gods, but was also a secular form avoiding the explicit use of Christian conceptions of deity. In contrast to the miracle plays, it used relatively few subjects from the Bible; in contrast to the morality plays, especially *Everyman*, it gave the teachings of the church a minor role. The figure of the proud cardinal, whose crimson robes make him a natural dramatic focus, is a popular symbol of the subordination of church to state. For the Elizabethans, the royal figure or human ruler tended to become the mythical centre of the action, and the relations of the ruler and his people take the place of the relations of gods and men.

The organizing conceptions of Elizabethan tragedy are the order of nature and the wheel of fortune. Nature as an order, though an order permeated with sin and death as a result of the fall of man, is the conception in Elizabethan drama corresponding to what we have called the ironic vision or being in time—Nietzsche's "Apollonian" vision. Fortune as a wheel rotated by the energy and ambition of man, which, however gigantic, can never get above a certain point, and consequently has to sink again, is the "Dionysian" or heroic vision which complements it. The order of nature provides the *data* of the human situation, the conditions man accepts by getting born. The wheel of fortune supplies the *facta*, what he contributes by his own energy and will.

But nature and fortune are not an antithesis: they interpenetrate in a very complex way. In the first place, there are

two levels of nature. Man lives in a lower nature, the physical
world or world of the four elements which moves in cycles.
This is particularly the Dionysian world of energy, and it is,
for practical purposes, identical with the wheel of fortune. A
state of aggressiveness, or what we now call the law of the
jungle, is "natural" to man, but natural only on this lower
level of nature. Above this world is a world of specifically
human nature, the world represented by the Christian paradise
and the Classical Golden Age, and symbolized by the starry
spheres with their heavenly music. Man lost this world with
the fall of Adam, but everything that is good for man, law,
virtue, education, religion, helps to raise him toward it again.
It is therefore also natural to man, on the higher level of
nature, to be civilized and in a state of social discipline. The
king or ruler symbolizes the invisible ideals of social discipline,
and the respect paid to him derives from those ideals. But
while he symbolizes them he does not incarnate them. No
earthly king is clear of the wheel of fortune, or independent of
the aggressive energy of the lower nature. He must know how
to wage war, how to punish, how to out-manœuvre the over-
ambitious. In *Richard II* the kingdom is symbolized by a
garden, and the garden, which is a state of art and a state of
nature at the same time, represents the upper human level of
nature. The gardener is addressed as "old Adam's likeness."
But the garden is not the garden of Eden; it is the garden that
"old" Adam was forced to cultivate after his fall, a garden
requiring constant effort and vigilance.

In contrast to most of his contemporaries (Chapman is the
chief exception), Shakespeare's sense of tragedy is deeply
rooted in history. *Richard II* and *Richard III* are nearly

identical with tragedy in form, and even when a history-play ends on a strong major chord it is never a comedy. The difference is chiefly that tragedy rounds off its action and history suggests a continuous story. We may compare the Greek dramatic tragedies with the Iliad, which, though complete in itself, is part of an epic cycle that keeps on going. As complete in itself, it is a tragedy, the tragedy of Hector; as part of the epic cycle, its central figure is Achilles, who does not die in the Iliad, but leaves us with a powerful intimation of mortality. Sometimes the continuity of history gives a cadence to a history-play that tragedy cannot achieve. *Henry V* ends with the conquest of France, just before Henry died and all his achievements began to vanish; *Henry VIII* ends with the triumph of Cranmer, Cromwell, and Anne Boleyn, along with the audience's knowledge of what soon happened to them. In other words, the history-play is more explicitly attached to the rotation of the wheel of fortune than the tragedy. But the difference is only one of degree: Fortinbras, Malcolm, perhaps Edgar, all provide some sense of "historical" continuity for their tragedies; we know what happens to Troy after the conclusion of *Troilus and Cressida*; Athens comes to terms with Alcibiades after the death of Timon, and the Roman plays are episodes of the continuing story of Rome.

The easiest way to get at the structure of Elizabethan tragedy is to think of it as a reversal of the structure of comedy. Comedy exhibits a type of action that I have elsewhere called a drive towards identity. This identity is of three kinds. There is plural or social identity, when a new social group crystallizes around the marriage of the hero and heroine in the final moments of the comedy. There is dual or erotic identity, when the hero and heroine get married. And there is individual identity, when a character comes to know himself in a way that he did not before, like Parolles, Angelo, or Katherina the shrew. Translating this division into tragic terms, there are three main kinds of tragic structure in Shakespeare and his contemporaries. There is, first, a social tragedy, with its roots in history, concerned with the fall of princes. There is, second, a tragedy that deals with the separation of lovers, the conflict of duty and passion, or the conflict of social and personal (sexual or family) interests. And there is, third, a tragedy in which the hero is removed from his social context, and is compelled to search for a purely individual identity. In Greek drama, these tragic structures might be called the Agamemnon type, the Antigone type, and the Oedipus type. In terms closer to Christianity, they might be called the tragedy of the killing of the father, the tragedy of the sacrifice of the son, and the tragedy of the isolation of the spirit. A critic who had learned his critical categories from Blake, like the present writer, would most naturally think of them as, respectively, tragedies of Urizen, tragedies of Luvah, and tragedies of Tharmas. In Shakespeare, we have a group of tragedies of order, *Julius Caesar*, *Macbeth*, and *Hamlet*; a group of tragedies of passion, *Romeo and Juliet*, *Antony and Cleopatra*, *Troilus and Cressida*, and *Coriolanus*; and a group of tragedies of isolation, *King Lear*, *Othello*, and *Timon of Athens*. These are not pigeon-holes, only different areas of emphasis; most of the plays have aspects that link them to all three groups. What seems a rather odd placing of *Othello* and *Coriolanus* should become clearer as we go on; *Titus Andronicus* belongs mainly to the first group. As passion or strong interest always conflicts either with another passion or with some externalized force, the passion-tragedy could also be called the dilemma-tragedy, as the example of *Antigone* indicates.

In each of Shakespeare's three social tragedies, *Julius Caesar*, *Macbeth*, and *Hamlet*, we have a tragic action based on three main character-groups. First is the order-figure: Julius Caesar in that play; Duncan in *Macbeth*; Hamlet's father. He is killed by a rebel-figure or usurper: Brutus and the other conspirators; Macbeth; Claudius. Third comes a nemesis-figure or nemesis-group: Antony and Octavius; Malcolm and Macduff; Hamlet. It is sometimes assumed that the hero, the character with the title-role, is always at the centre of the play, and that all plays are to be related in the same way to the hero; but each of the heroes of these three tragedies belongs to a different aspect of the total action. The nemesis-figure is partly a revenger and partly an avenger. He is primarily obsessed with killing the rebel-figure, but he has a secondary function of restoring something of the previous order.

The Elizabethan social or historical tragedy shows, much more clearly than the other two kinds, the impact of heroic energy on the human condition, the wheel of fortune creaking against the greater wheel of nature. Central to the form is an Elizabethan assumption about society, which is simple but takes some historical imagination to grasp. Society to the Elizabethans was a structure of personal authority, with the ruler at its head, and a personal chain of authority extending from the ruler down. Everybody had a superior, and this fact, negatively, emphasized the limited and finite nature of the human situation. Positively, the fact that the ruler was an individual with a personality was what enabled his subjects to be individuals and to have personalities too. The man who possesses the secret and invisible virtues of human nature is the man with the quiet mind, so celebrated in Elizabethan lyric poetry. But such a man is dependent on the ceaseless vigilance of the ruler for his peace.

This view of social order, with its stress on the limited, the finite, and the individual, corresponds, as indicated above, to Nietzsche's Apollonian vision in Greek culture. That makes it hard for us to understand it. We ourselves live in a Dionysian society, with mass movements sweeping across it, leaders rising and falling, and constantly taking the risk of being dissolved into a featureless tyranny where all sense of the individual disappears. We even live on a Dionysian earth, staggering drunkenly around the sun. The treatment of the citizens in *Julius Caesar* and *Coriolanus* puzzles us: we are apt to feel that Shakespeare's attitude is anti-democratic, instead of recognizing that the situation itself is pre-democratic. In my own graduate-student days during the nineteen-thirties, there appeared an Orson Welles adaptation of *Julius Caesar* which required the hero to wear a fascist uniform and pop his eyes like Mussolini, and among students there was a good deal of discussion about whether Shakespeare's portrayal of, say, Coriolanus showed "fascist tendencies" or not. But fascism is a disease of democracy: the fascist leader is a demagogue, and a demagogue is precisely what Coriolanus is not. The demagogues in that play are the tribunes whom the people have chosen as their own managers. The people in Shakespeare constitute a "Dionysian" energy in society: that is, they represent nothing but a potentiality of response to leadership.

We are apt to assume, like Brutus, that leadership and freedom threaten one another, but, for us as for Shakespeare, there is no freedom without the sense of the individual, and in the tragic vision, at least, the leader or hero is the primary and original individual. The good leader individualizes his followers; the tyrant or bad leader intensifies mass energy into a mob. Shakespeare has grasped the ambiguous nature of Dionysus in a way that Nietzsche (like D. H. Lawrence later) misses. In no period of history does Dionysus have anything to do with freedom; his function is to release us from the burden of freedom. The last thing the mob says in both *Julius Caesar* and *Coriolanus* is pure Dionysus: "Tear him to pieces."

Two contemporary plays, much simpler in their construction than any of Shakespeare's, illustrate the impact of the *facta* of fortune on the *data* of nature. At one extreme we have Marlowe's Tamburlaine, who is the Dionysian energy of fortune incarnate. Tamburlaine is a "scourge of God," conquering one demoralized society after another with nothing in the order of nature to stop him: nothing, that is, except death itself. He is a portent of the kind of limitless ferocity that would get loose if the alliance of social and natural order represented by the strong ruler were to break down. At the opposite extreme (perhaps designed to be that) we have Chapman's double play on the conspiracy and tragedy of Byron. Here the central figure is an idealized Henry IV of France, a firm, wise, patient ruler who has to deal with the excessive ambition and egotism of one of his subjects. He gives Byron every chance to fit into the social order, and only when forbearance becomes obviously impossible does he reluctantly consent to Byron's execution. One scene consists of a reported speech by Elizabeth I, and Essex is mentioned more than once in the dialogue, so it is clear that Henry IV is not the only ideal monarch in Europe. Henry and Elizabeth are what we have called order-figures, rulers whose personalities give form and shape to their kingdoms. Byron, along with Tamburlaine, is a rebel-figure: whatever his moral status he is a genuine hero, and everything about him suggests the unbounded and infinite, just as everything about the order-figure suggests law, finiteness, and the principle of individuality.

In Shakespeare's day there had been no permanently success-ful example of popular sovereignty. Machiavelli had drawn the conclusion that there were two forms of government: popular governments, which were unstable, and principalities, or what we should call dictatorships, the stability of which depended on the force and cunning of the prince. This analysis, of course, horrified the idealists of the sixteenth century who were trying to rationalize the government of the prince with arguments about the "general good," and so Machiavelli became, by way of the attacks on him, a conven-tional bogey of Elizabethan drama. From the point of view of tragic structure, what Machiavelli was doing was destroying the integrity of tragedy by obliterating the difference between the order-figure and the rebel-figure. Machiavelli comes into Marlowe's *Jew of Malta* to speak the prologue, and there he asks: "What right had Caesar to the empire?"—in itself surely a fair enough question, and one which expresses the central issue in the tragedy of order.

The order-figure, in Shakespeare, holds his position through a subtle combination of *de jure* and *de facto* authority. In the history plays, legitimacy is a factor of great importance: a magical aura surrounds the rightful heir, and the favour of

God, or at least the co-operation of nature, seems bound up with preserving the line of succession. It is clear that hereditary succession is regarded as essential to a fully developed social order. Richard II was an impossible king, but Bolingbroke's seizure of the crown was an awful and portentous event, throwing a shadow over the whole Lancastrian line. It does not affect Henry V, apparently, because he succeeded his father in good faith, but it brings disaster as soon as he dies. In the first part of *Henry VI* we are told something which is played down in the later histories: that Bolingbroke not only took the crown from the Lord's anointed, but pushed the person next in line, the Earl of Mortimer, out of the way. In trying to determine the moral boundary between the ruthless-ness of Henry V or Henry VIII and the rascality of John or Richard III, the attempts of the latter two to get rid of the heir apparent are clearly decisive. Bolingbroke, though he wanted Richard II murdered, has to dissociate himself from the actual deed by making a scapegoat out of Exton: in *King John* it is insisted that Hubert is "damned" if he really killed Arthur. Still, John, like Richard III and Macbeth, was simply accepting the logic of the *de jure* argument, which implies that anyone who has any claim to the throne at all can acquire the *de jure* aura by murdering everybody who has a better claim. To some extent this is true—that is, it is to some extent accepted by Shakespeare as a dramatic postulate. Once Arthur is dead, the legitimate heir becomes John's son, the young Henry III, and the fortune of England is bound up with recognizing him as such. In plays where leadership does not depend wholly on hereditary succession, as in the Roman plays and *Hamlet*, the choice of a predecessor, including Caesar's preference for Antony and Hamlet's for Fortinbras, has a good deal of moral significance. Enough is said, however, about the merits and services of Coriolanus, Othello, Caesar, Titus, and others to make it obvious that in some social contexts *de jure* authority can be earned as well as inherited.

Richard II was a lawful king, but a mediaeval king was perennially short of money, and if he were extravagant or a poor manager he had to live practically like a brigand in the middle of his own society. In this situation the question of what kind of law the lawful king represents becomes very ambiguous. The success of Bolingbroke's rebellion depends partly on its justice: he makes common cause with those plundered by Richard's favourites. The justice he appeals to is the right of inheriting private property: a dramatist who could write a whole play about King John without mentioning Magna Carta could hardly have cared less about the freedom that broadens through precedents. But Bolingbroke's real success lies in, so to speak, the nature of nature. Richard is the natural head of the state, but has not done a ruler's work, and society's need for a centre of order throws up a natural force in the form of Bolingbroke. One does not feel either that Bolingbroke is a pawn of circumstances or that he is consumed by personal ambition: one feels that he is part of a process too much in accord with nature to be described even by such a mysterious term as fate. Shakespeare presents him rather as Marvell was later to present Oliver Cromwell:

> Nature that hateth emptiness
> Allows of penetration less,
>   And therefore must make room
>   Where greater spirits come.

Richard is king *de jure*; Bolingbroke is the power *de facto*, but at a certain point the *de facto* power acquires the *de jure* attribute as well: this point is represented by York's dramatic transfer of loyalties. We are not dealing in this play with a simple moral issue: Bolingbroke is neither a wicked usurper like Macbeth nor a righteous avenger like Richmond. Both his supporter Northumberland and his opponent Carlisle are right in their attitudes. Julius Caesar has no *de jure* monarch to displace, but he comes to power in the same way, through society's need for a personal leader.

The ruler, we said, represents, though he does not embody, the upper order of nature, the world man was originally intended to live in. The conventional physical symbol of this order is that of the starry spheres with their unheard music. The music is that of the Apollonian world, for Apollo was the god of music, at least of the music that suggests "harmony," order, and stability. Nietzsche's Dionysian conception of music belongs to the age of Wagner. Metaphors of harmony are seldom far away from any discussion of social order, and the passing of such an order is regularly symbolized by music. This is true even of the fall of Catherine of Aragon in *Henry VIII*. The deposed Richard II is poet, actor, and musician, and when he hears music and remarks,

> How sour sweet music is
> When time is broke and no proportion kept!

he goes on to make it clear that the words "time" and "proportion" link music and social order together.

Closely allied to this use of music is the suggestion of the supernatural. Ghosts, omens, portents, oracles, magic, witchcraft do not enter tragedy primarily as marvels: they are not there to be exhilarating, in the way that they are in romance.

As things experienced, they threaten our sense of reality with madness: as things conceived, they show up the limited and finite nature of the human perspective, especially in thought. Thus they emphasize the existential irony in tragedy by showing that there are always more things to be experienced in heaven and earth than philosophy can digest. The authority of the order-figure is attached to a mysterious and invisible nature of which we know little except that it has authority, and, in Shakespearean tragedy, it is usually only the ruler's ghost that walks. Except for the episode of Hercules leaving Antony, where mysterious music is again heard, there is nothing really supernatural in Shakespeare's tragedies that is not connected with the murder of the order-figures. In *Macbeth* we have Banquo's ghost instead of Duncan's, partly because of the emphasis on the repose that Duncan has gained by getting murdered, and partly because the line of the reigning monarch descends from Banquo. The scene in which Duncan makes Malcolm Prince of Cumberland in front of Macbeth is oddly anticipatory of the scene in *Paradise Lost* in which God the Father arouses the jealousy of Satan by displaying his Son, and it is interesting that Milton considered writing a *Macbeth* which would include the ghost of Duncan. The special case of the ghosts in *Richard III* will meet us later. The physical symbol of order is that of the stars in their courses: rebellion is symbolized by comets, thunder and lightning, "exhalations," and similar aspects of meteorology unusual enough to be called unnatural, because they interrupt the sense of nature as predictable.

Elizabethan tragedy, while it may in some respects be Senecan, is certainly not Stoic. The Stoic's primary loyalty is a loyalty of conviction to the universal law of nature and to humanity as a whole. In Shakespeare and his contemporaries what commands loyalty is a specific social order embodied in a specific person. In the histories there is no conception of any loyalty broader than England, and even when Shakespeare's subject is the Roman Empire in which Stoicism grew up, loyalties are still concrete and personal. It is a *comitatus* group that gathers around both Caesar and Antony. In the tragedies, as in the comedies, Shakespeare's settings are deliberately archaic. The form of society in them is closer to that of the Iliad, or of *Beowulf*, than it is to ours—or to his own. The social unit involved may be a great kingdom—England or France or the Roman Empire—but its head and eyes, to use images very frequently employed, are the ruler and his small select band of personal followers. Warfare, again, continually breaks down into the warfare of the Iliad: physical prowess by individual heroes fighting in pairs. Coriolanus has no sense whatever of what Ulysses calls "the still and mental parts" of battle: he simply dashes in and fights with his own hands. The histories ignore the more realistic side of mediaeval warfare, the side that was essentially a ransom racket. The collapse of this sense of personal heroism, as in Achilles' murder of Hector or Octavius' contemptuous refusal of Antony's challenge, indicates the subsiding of the tragic into the ironic vision. The role of religion also is Homeric. Prayer in Homer consists mainly of reminding the gods pointedly that they have been well fed by a hero's sacrifices, and that victory in battle is the obvious way of making sure that the supply does not fail. Similarly, the God of Shakespeare's histories ignores the pleas of the afflicted, but appears to respond eagerly to Henry's suggestion that he will do "more" than the two chantries he has already built for King Richard's soul if he wins Agincourt.

Brutus in *Julius Caesar* is something of a Stoic, even though it is Cassius who calls himself one, and Brutus is one of the few characters in Shakespeare capable of an impersonal loyalty. But Brutus is utterly lost in the Elizabethan Rome that Shakespeare depicts. He assumes that the process of leadership looks after itself, and that his only task is to remove the danger of tyranny. Consequently he is helpless in the face of Antony, who understands the principle of personal leadership. Cassius, in contrast, is motivated in his hatred of Caesar by personal feelings; because they are personal they are concrete, and because they are concrete he can see clearly what has to be done to consolidate power. But he is emotionally dependent on Brutus: that is, his loyalties, like his resentments, are personal, and Brutus is the one man for whom personal loyalties are inappropriate. Enobarbus in *Antony and Cleopatra* shows the existential nature of tragedy even more clearly. He attempts a kind of intellectual detachment that would rationalize his leaving a losing cause and joining one that seems more in accord with the laws of nature and the general good of humanity. After all, nobody can think of Mark Antony as the Lord's anointed. But Enobarbus' own nature and humanity are bound up with his personal loyalty to Antony and to Cleopatra—for it is only when Cleopatra seems about to betray Antony that he gives in to his impulse to desert. Once he has exchanged a loyalty of experience for a loyalty of rational conviction, however, and compares his detachment with Antony's generosity, he is too numbed even to feel like a traitor. He feels simply that he is no longer alive, and he does not have to kill himself: he merely lies down and dies.

An equally instructive figure outside Shakespeare is Clermont, the hero of Chapman's second Bussy play. Clermont believes himself to be a Stoic hero, invulnerable to the blows of fate, his soul in accord with the laws of nature, an indestructible centre for his own universe. He holds forth on these subjects at considerable length to anyone who will listen, and as a good many people are compelled to listen, the play develops into quite a Stoical harangue. Clermont, however, is a protégé of the Duke of Guise, hence his loyalties, and therefore his real existence, are bound up with that Duke, whom he supports to the point of defending the St. Bartholomew Day massacre in front of an Elizabethan audience that was at least half Protestant. When the Duke is assassinated, Clermont commits suicide, describing himself as the Duke's "creature" after having all but convinced us that he is a creature of universal law. True, an exalted notion of friendship is a central aspect of that law, but what the action really shows us is a philosophy blown to pieces by the existential facts of murder, irrational loyalty, and revenge.

A loyalty like this brings us very close to the spirit of the real Machiavelli, who found the source of social stability in a ruling personality and who recognized that the qualities of leadership were not moral. In Shakespeare there are, in practice, certain moral limits to leadership: an undying loyalty to Macbeth or Richard III would be quixotic. But theoretically there are no limits. Bosola in Webster's *Duchess of Malfi* reminds us of this when he remarks that it is no harm to die

in so good a quarrel, after he has wiped out practically the
whole cast as a result of being the loyal "creature" of two
desperately wicked men. The strength of personal loyalty
accounts not only for so many suicides in Elizabethan tragedy,
or attempted suicides like Horatio's, but also for the irresistible
power of the motivation for revenge. Brutus predicts that as
Antony is Julius Caesar's creature, he cannot survive Caesar's
death as an effective force. This is typical of the way that
Brutus misinterprets political facts: Antony's single-minded
desire to revenge Caesar makes him immensely stronger than
Brutus.

One of the most familiar facts of Elizabethan tragedy is that
revenge is so often presented as a duty, a moral imperative, the
very call of conscience itself, and may still be so even if the
avenger is a ferocious sadist who thoroughly enjoys what he
is doing. The sanctions of religion often endorse the revenge,
and the audience is usually assumed to be sympathetic to it.
If Desdemona had been sleeping with Cassio, we (that is, most
people in most audiences including Shakespeare's) might still
think that Othello's murder of her was wrong, but certainly
Othello would not have thought so, and the other characters
would have taken, not our view, but the view of the tragic
convention. Hamlet believes that "heaven was ordinant" in
seeing to it that Rosencrantz and Guildenstern were killed
without "shriving-time allowed." They were merely serving
the king whom they had every reason to believe was the rightful king, but this time the convention is pulling in the opposite
direction. Hamlet, again, is less remorseful about killing
Polonius than annoyed with Polonius for not being Claudius,
and seems genuinely bewildered that Laertes should be hostile

to him. He can only realize, by an effort of which he is rather proud, that Laertes too might want to avenge a father's murder:

> For, by the image of my cause, I see
> The portraiture of his.

We should say that Hamlet at this point was completely paranoid, and in fact Hamlet also blames his madness when apologizing to Laertes for having exterminated his family. But the sanctity of the greater revenge atones for everything: Laertes dies full of remorse for his own treachery and flights of angels sing Hamlet to his rest.

In Shakespearean tragedy, man is not really man until he has entered what is called a social contract, when he ceases to be a "subject" in the philosophical sense and becomes a subject in the political one, essentially related to his society. The ordered society in Shakespeare is, to use Heidegger's term, ecstatic: its members are outside themselves, at work in the world, and their being is their function. As we saw, the vital thread of Enobarbus' life was the tie that bound him to Antony, not anything inside himself. What Falstaff sardonically notes of the relation of Shallow to his servants could in other contexts be quite seriously true: "Their spirits are so married in conjunction with the participation of society that they flock together in consent, like so many wild-geese." In the first part of *Henry VI*, Talbot, the hero of the play, is kidnapped by a French Countess, who says to him:

> Long time thy shadow hath been thrall to me,
> For in my gallery thy picture hangs:
> But now the substance shall endure the like,
> And I will chain these legs and arms of thine.

Talbot tells her that in seizing him she still has only the shadow, for "his substance, sinews, arms and strength" consist of the soldiers who follow him.

It follows that, for the leader, there is no difference between reality and appearance, between what he is and what he seems to be. His reality is his appearance, and what he does is what he is. Machiavelli remarks that it is not important that a prince should be virtuous, only that he should seem so. Until we stop to think about it, it is difficult to realize how far this principle goes in Shakespeare. Edward IV was the first to stab Prince Edward on the field of Tewkesbury, and he condemned his brother Clarence to death out of a superstitious fear of his name, influenced by his mistress. Yet, had it not been for the villainy of Gloucester, Edward would have got away with what is practically a saint's death, mourned by his faithful queen. The piety of Henry VI, on the other hand, was genuine, and therefore contemptible, because it prevented him from being a sufficiently ruthless ruler.

The prince is a *dramatic* figure: like the actor, he is required not so much to be as to appear, to put on a show. The conception of reputation in Shakespeare is bound up with the emphasis on appearance. It seems selfish for Hamlet to prevent Horatio's suicide, not because he cares about Horatio's life, but because he wants somebody to survive to tell his story properly. It seems weak in Othello, as Eliot says, to beg that a story of his killing an anti-Venetian Turk should be told about him. It seems cowardly for Cleopatra to be motivated to suicide, and Macbeth to his final hopeless fight with Macduff, out of a fear of being publicly ridiculed. But for successful rulers, how they appear in society is their real existence, and it is natural that a sense of an original function should appear like a mirage to these tragic figures in the last moments of their isolation and failure. At the end of *Hamlet* we get a strong feeling that the play we are watching is, in a sense, Horatio's story, and this feeling links together the two conceptions of reputation as the real personality and of the actor as the real man.

The good ruler is not, clearly, the ruler who performs good acts, but the ruler who does what has to be done at the time. The word "time" is very important here, and we shall return to it. Ruling involves a good deal of killing and executing, assaulting other countries when they are in a weak spot, committing minor injustices for the sake of greater ends. *De jure* authority is of little importance without *de facto* power, and the basis of *de facto* power is the ordeal by battle, the symbol of which appears at the beginning of *Richard II* in connection with Bolingbroke. The good ruler, in short, is the ruler who wins his battles. *Henry V* is a very complex play, but all its complexities do not eliminate from it the simple-minded glorification of the victory of Agincourt, and the conquest of France. It is in the exhilaration of this victory that England, in all its history, comes nearest to feeling its social identity. The feeling seems to depend on two elements to be found only on a battlefield: the presence of death and the inspiring power of enmity. In contrast to hatred, which is divisive, enmity is a socially unifying force. Two servants in *Coriolanus* agree that while war creates enmity, it is peace that breeds hatred, because then "men have less need of one another," and one thinks of Falstaff's chilling phrase about the men he recruits: "the cankers of a calm world and a long peace." The leader who has the authority to expose his followers to death is the leader who commands loyalty. Timon tries to build up a peaceful society on a basis of equality, generosity, and mutual friendship, and sees it instantly disintegrate in front of him.

In the Folio text of *Julius Caesar*, Caesar makes a vague boast that he "doth not wrong": what he originally said, according to Ben Jonson, was: "Caesar did never wrong, but with just cause." Jonson thought this ridiculous, but the fact that one may do wrong with just cause is central to the whole paradox of ruling, and it is highly characteristic of Shakespeare's Caesar that he had the insight to see this. For Shakespeare's Caesar was in a position to answer Machiavelli's question in Marlowe about his right to the empire. The answer is not the simple one that might is right, but still less is it the idealistic one that might imitates right. The ruler is not, like the judge, a mere incarnation of law: he is a personality, and in tragedy the personality takes precedence over whatever is conceptual or moral. If we start with the view that the head of the state should be an instrument of law or a philosopher-king, we shall end with disillusioned reflections about the little wisdom with which the world is governed. In Shakespeare's histories and tragedies the world is not governed by wisdom at all, but by personal will. For Shakespeare's order-figures it would be more accurate to say that right imitates might. The process of holding power, however ruthless, is primary; whatever order and justice and stability there may be follow after that.

It is easy to infer from all this that Shakespeare was a great "believer" in personal rule, and wanted his audience to believe in it too: that he idealized strong rulers and minimized their faults, glorified the successful military leader and admired ruthlessness and hardness. The Roman leaders are much more attractive in him than they are in Plutarch. One could quote a good deal in support of this thesis and still misinterpret the poet. The poet presents a vision of society: the critic, in trying to interpret the vision, is almost compelled to translate it into a conception or theory of society. As a theory of society, what we have been expounding sounds rather childish, especially to people who, like ourselves, live in a post-tragic age. For us, to put a personal loyalty above a loyalty of principle, as the Nazis did, is culturally regressive: it begins in hysteria and ends in psychosis. But Shakespeare has no theory of society: what he has is a vision of society, and that vision is so powerfully convincing that we accept it without question. We often think of Shakespeare's tragedies as reflecting the social facts of his own age, but, as already indicated, they do this only to a very limited extent. The settings of *King Lear, Macbeth, Hamlet, Coriolanus* are primitive by Elizabethan standards too, and because they are primitive they are archetypal, reflecting the immutable facts of passion and power and loyalty and absurdity that are always present in human life. The vision in Shakespeare's tragedies is, quite simply, a tragic vision, a vision in which death is the end of all action, and in which the actions that lead most directly to death are the strongest ones. The wise man, says Socrates the philosopher, will live by the laws of the just state whatever state he is living in. Every man, says the tragic dramatist, lives, or would like to live, by the self-destroying passions that are most clearly revealed in the archaic settings of Shakespeare's tragedies.

In the three plays that are typically tragedies of order, the order-figure is murdered fairly soon. Hamlet's father is killed before the play begins; Duncan just as he is about to enjoy some of the fruits of victory; Caesar just before he accepts the kingship and enters into his *de jure* heritage. No actual ruler is outside the operation of the wheel of fortune, and no triumph therefore can be without its reminders of death. The Ides of March come for Caesar; Duncan is saved from the treachery of the Thane of Cawdor by the Thane's more treacherous successor; and on the great day of the senior Hamlet's life, when he won his duel with the King of Norway and Prince Hamlet was born, the first grave-digger entered into his occupation. But the simple irony of fortune's turning wheel is not the real dramatic point of these assassinations. Critics who have noted that Aristotle's word "hamartia" is also the ordinary New Testament word for sin have often assumed that a tragic victim must have a "flaw" or a "proud mind" that will make his death morally intelligible. But the flaw of the murdered ruler is simply to be there, and his proud mind is merely to be what he is. Unlike Edward IV, who imprisoned his brother because his name began with G, Caesar dismisses the warning soothsayer as a "dreamer." Caesar's "flaw," then, is only that he fails to be a superstitious tyrant. As for pride of mind, even Caesar hardly has that in an excessive degree, much less the "meek" Duncan. The fall of the prince may have a moral cause, but the cause is not primary: what is primary is the event. Or rather, not only the event, but the event along with its consequences. The important thing about the order-figure, in short, is not that he gets murdered, but that he *has been* murdered. The essential tragic action starts just after his death. This is also true of the action of *King Lear*, where the order-figure, by abdicating as king, has destroyed his own social context, and has therefore essentially murdered himself.

The pushing back of the murder of the ruler into something pre-tragic is closely connected with a prominent feature in the histories: the tendency to idealize an earlier age. The story of the War of the Roses in *Henry VI* looks back longingly to the great days of Agincourt and laments the premature death of Henry V. But there were conspiracies against Henry V, as well as against his father, which looked back to the deposition of Richard II as the beginning of all social evils. We go back to Richard's time, and find John of Gaunt idealizing an age which ended with Edward III. There is a trace of the same feeling at the opening of *Julius Caesar*, with the tribune's despairing cry: "Knew ye not Pompey?" We are back to the point at which we began. The heroic has been; only the human is. It is the same feeling that gives the lost cause its glamour: the feeling that paints Oliver Cromwell with the wart on his nose and gives Charles I all the Van Dykes. As we continue to study the romantic appeal of the lost cause, it begins to attach itself to the dream of a lost paradise or golden age. For, as Proust tells us, all paradises are paradises that we have lost; all social ideals are ideals that no longer exist; justice itself, considered as an ideal, vanished long ago with Astraea.

Poetry must have an image; drama must have a character, and the feeling of lost social identity is what is expressed in the story of the fallen prince. The fallen prince is the "primal father" of a rather desperate myth of Freud's, which seems to assume a crude notion of a "collective unconscious" that literary criticism, fortunately, does not need. In criticism, the murdered prince, from Agamemnon onwards, stands for the sense of falling away from social unity which is constantly present in every generation. The tragic vision begins with being in time, and time is always time *after*. It is always later than a time when we had a greater allowance of life and could attach more significance in that life to parental figures. Or, reversing the image, we now watch a heroic action with what is described by Lewis of France in *King John* as:

> those baby eyes
> That never saw the giant world enraged.

We have frequently mentioned Richard II, and we notice that Richard uses several phrases linking his deposition to the trial of Christ. The primary reason for this is that Richard has one of the essential characteristics of royalty, being a born actor, and Bolingbroke can steal his crown but not his show. He adopts these parallels, not because he is a Christ-like character, but because he fancies himself in that role. And yet his dramatic instinct is sound. As king, Richard has "lost the hearts" of both nobles and commons, and so for all practical purposes has abdicated his birthright. As a man, he attracts the same mixture of sympathy and condemnation as any other man who has muffed a very important job. But purely as lost cause, as a symbol of man's rejection of the Lord's anointed, he is entitled to his echoes. Behind the echoes of the rejected Christ are the echoes of the lost paradise itself, for, as the Queen says in the garden scene, Richard's fall is "a second fall of cursed man." Every fall of every ruler is that.

There are, then, two symbolic aspects of the ruler, or what we have been calling the order-figure, in Shakespeare's tragedies. There is the deposed or murdered ruler, Caesar, Duncan, Hamlet's father, Richard II, the abdicating Lear, who, as that, represents a lost social identity: we shall not look upon his like again, or the like of what he stood for. His archetype is neither Apollo nor Dionysus, but Keats's hero Hyperion, the father of the sun-god, to whom Hamlet's father is twice compared. The other is the ruler conceived as actual ruler, the successful strong man, Octavius, Henry V, Henry VIII, and Julius Caesar for the first two acts of his play. Such a figure is both Apollo and Dionysus, lord of both the order of nature and the heroic energy of fortune. The leader controls a world where reality is also appearance, and therefore illusion, as well as reality. Nietzsche points out how the defining of individuality, which is the key to Apollonian order, is only made possible by continuous illusion. The social order the leader represents grows by conquest and successful battles; sanity depends on hysteria; law and stability depend on punishment. His palace is founded on a prison, as Henry V unconsciously indicates:

> We are no tyrant, but a Christian king;
> Unto whose grace our passion is as subject
> As is our wretches fettered in our prisons.

The strong ruler is in the position that Camus in our day has identified with Sisyphus, forever condemned to roll the stone of time. A ruler who has been killed at the height of his powers, or is thought of as living a long time ago, like the Edward the Confessor of *Macbeth* who could heal the sick, may become a legend of mystery and magic, a dream of glory that is hardly a memory and has ceased to be a hope. His legend becomes, like the ghost of the murdered Caesar to Brutus at Philippi, the symbol of our own evil genius, of our inability to reach our own ideals. Polite fictions about the present, such as the implicit reference to James I in the *Macbeth* passage, or Cranmer's prophecy at the end of *Henry VIII*, turn the tragic vision into something else. The tragic present is always in the intervening rebel state. And so every actual strong ruler, as that, is something of an avenger or nemesis, someone who re-establishes and renews a legendary glory in a spirit of wrath. The more successful he is, the more his order appears to be an emergency order, proved in war, which is, as Henry V says, the vengeance of God. Then the strong ruler in his turn passes into legend and his achievements into nothing.

In the total action of *Hamlet* there are three concentric tragic spheres, each with a murdered father and a nemesis. At the centre is Polonius, murdered by accident and avenged by his son. Around this comes the main action of the play, where Hamlet's father is murdered and avenged by his son. Around this again comes the story of the old and the young Fortinbras of Norway, the father slain by Hamlet's father, the son achieving by accident what a successful revenge would have achieved, the throne of Denmark. Of Fortinbras we know little except that he will fight for anything; so whatever the future of Denmark may be, it is unlikely to be a peaceful future. The story of Polonius, Laertes, and the mad Ophelia is an ironic tragedy of blood, some features of which we shall look at next. The story of the old and the young Fortinbras gives to the whole action the dimension of being in time, the turning of the wheel of history. In between comes the story of Hamlet, Hamlet whose mind is a complete universe in itself, ranging from hints of a divinity that shapes our ends to a melancholy sense of the unbearable loathsomeness of physical life, and whose actions range from delicate courtesy to shocking brutality. All this magnificent vision of heroic energy is poured out as a sacrifice to a dead father, to a ghost who returns screaming for blood from what is supposed to be a place of purification. Hamlet is forced to strike everything out of his "tables" that represents thought and feeling and observation and awareness, and concentrate solely on hatred and revenge, a violent alteration of his natural mental habits that makes his assuming of madness only partly voluntary. It is the paradox of tragedy that he shows us infinitely more than hatred and revenge, that he could never have shown it without the impulse to revenge, and that nothing is left of it except silence for him and the telling of his story for us.

The tailors of
the earth:
The tragedy
of passion

The tailors of the earth: The tragedy of passion

In the tragedy of order a strong and capable ruler is murdered, this act and the revenge for it occupying the major part of the tragic action. In such a tragedy the ruler himself has to be a mature man in middle life, and the rebel-figure who strikes him down has to be of comparable weight. Brutus, Macbeth, and Claudius are all well past their youth and solidly married, and are in an almost fraternal relation to their victims, especially Claudius, whose crime, as he recognizes, belongs to the archetype of Cain. The tragedy of order is thus one form of a struggle-of-brothers theme which is frequent in the histories as well. Richard III and John are brothers of the monarchs they succeed by usurpation; Prince Henry and Hotspur have the same name and are the same age, twins struggling in the womb of time, like Esau and Jacob.

In the tragedy of order the ruler's authority is a "good" thing only in the sense that society is not demonstrably any better off without it. Brutus' crucial error, we said, lay in his assumption that the problem of authority takes care of itself: that if we remove the threat of Caesar we need not worry too much about the succession to Caesar. This error is symbolized by his dissuading the conspirators from taking an oath. The oath would have consolidated a revolutionary group, which could then have acted with the same ruthless efficiency as the second triumvirate (or two-thirds of it) does later. But it is obviously possible to construct a tragedy in which the order itself is evil, and in which the rebellion against it appeals to the sympathy of the audience. This is the rule in the type of tragedy usually described as the tragedy of blood, though I should prefer to call it the tragedy of the sick society. In, for instance, *The Spanish Tragedy*, *The Revenger's Tragedy*, *The White Devil*, or *Women Beware Women*, we are introduced to a society, usually a court, so hopelessly rotten and corrupt that we can expect from it nothing but a long series of treacherous murders. There is no order-figure: the head of the state is as bad as everyone else, and the only action we feel much in sympathy with is that of revenge—revenge on him, usually. In a society that is evil, cruel, sick or repressive, the hero is likely to be crushed simply because he is a hero. In the tragedies of order the action focusses on a rebel whose fortune is too big for nature. In tragedies of a sick society the central figure is often a victim, and the victim's nature is too big for his fortune. What is squeezed out of the tragic action is not excessive ambition but excessive vitality, though it is only because of the perverted social context that it is excessive.

Chapman's Byron plays, we said, are examples of a tragedy of order in which the order-figure is idealized, and the authority he represents is consequently idealized too. In *Bussy d'Ambois* the situation is very different: here the setting is the weak and divided court of Henry III of France. Bussy is a force of nature, recalling, as an admirer says, the Golden Age, imported into this court, where his energy and outspokenness, together with his duelling prowess, proceed to tear it to pieces until he is done to death. A weak society has little to do with either the order of nature or the wheel of fortune, as it is neither natural nor fortunate, and a hero in such a setting has about him the energy of an unspoiled nature, which in that context is destructive. Such a play is an order-tragedy in reverse, as it were, in which the rebel-figure has our sympathy. *The Duchess of Malfi* is even more clearly a tragedy of unspoiled vitality crushed by an evil society. The excuse for murdering the Duchess is that she has polluted the aristocracy by marrying someone of healthier blood, but the real reason is that she is young, attractive, and warm-hearted, all qualities that infuriate her psychotic brothers.

The killing of the order-figure relates itself to the theme of the primal father. Therefore the tragedy of the destruction of vitality in a sick society may easily become the tragedy of youth, where the order-figure is an evil father-figure and the victim is typically a son or daughter in revolt against him. The clearest example of such a tragedy in English literature is Shelley's *Cenci.* Here the essential theme is the struggle of youth and age, with the sadistic and incestuous Cenci representing both fatherhood and evil. Two spheres of repressive authority enfold him: one is that of the Church, represented by the Pope, who takes his side primarily because he stands for the tyranny of fatherhood; the other is that of history and tradition, the temporal chain of repression that only revolution can break, a revolution of which Beatrice is a portent. For Shelley, tyranny and repression are essentially a part of the *data* of existence, the state of things associated with Jupiter in *Prometheus Unbound.* There is no tragedy of this type in Shakespeare. Apart from the resistance of Cordelia in the

opening scene of *King Lear*, the nearest approach to it is
Romeo and Juliet, where our sympathies are so solidly with
the young lovers. Yet nobody would say that the Prince or
the parental figures in that play were evil or sinister: the most
sinister character is Tybalt, and he has more in common with
the "angry boys" of Elizabethan London. But the feud of
course is evil, and the lovers are sacrificial victims of it: they
are described by Capulet as "Poor sacrifices of our enmity,"
and the prologue speaks of

> the continuance of their parents' rage,
> Which, but their children's end, nought could remove.

The feeling of the sinister and repressive is really transferred
in this play from the parental figures to the order of nature
which, as we saw, is closely connected with the order of
society. The sense of a fateful order symbolized by the "inaus-
picious stars" dominates *Romeo and Juliet*, though it is rare
in Shakespeare as a whole.

Tragedies based on the rebellion of youth against age are
not frequent in the drama of Shakespeare's time: even the
Duchess of Malfi is killed by brothers. The central action of
The Spanish Tragedy is the treacherous murder of young
Horatio, whose dialogue with Bel-imperia has a gentle elegiac
melancholy about it in contrast to the pervading air of bloody
bustle in the rest of the play. Horatio is a martyred son, a kind
of Absalom-figure, described by his father as "a youth run
through and through with villains' swords, hanging upon this
tree." But the father is the avenger of the murder, not the
cause of it. In Shakespeare there are no Absalom-figures, but
we notice that under a tyrant's rule, when social order does
become corrupt, dramatic interest often focusses sharply, if

briefly, on a youthful victim: the princes in the Tower, Arthur in *King John*, Macduff's little boy in *Macbeth*. Such figures are most conspicuous in the earliest plays. In the Greeks and in Seneca much attention is paid to youthful sacrificial victims: those who, like Iphigeneia, Polyxena, or Astyanax, are murdered to appease a wrathful deity or the ghosts of the dead. *Titus Andronicus*, though without any historical roots, is an intensely academic play, full of explicit literary allusions, some of which, such as Lavinia's reading of the story of Philomela in Ovid, form part of the action, and the play glances at many of the stock Classical themes, like that of the unburied body. We notice that the first action of the play is the sacrifice of a boy, Alarbus, and from this action all the horrors of the play take their origin. Alarbus is avenged by his mother Tamora, and her revenge is associated in the dialogue with that of Hecuba. Again, in the first part of *Henry VI*, the hero Talbot sees his young son killed before his face, and compares him to the youthful victim-figure Icarus, and himself to Daedalus, escaping by their death from a world that Suffolk later describes as a "labyrinth" "where Minotaurs and ugly treasons lurk." The gloomy action goes on until it winds up at the end of Part Three with the murder, first of the young Prince Edward, then of his father Henry VI, who again compares himself to Daedalus and his son to Icarus.

We have emphasized the way in which most of Shakespeare's tragic characters are in an "ecstatic" relation to their societies: their life is in their social relationships, and their loyalties are personal. In some of the tragedies, notably *Romeo and Juliet*, *Troilus and Cressida*, and *Antony and Cleopatra*, the social order is split, and there is no symbol or centre of social unity. Verona is torn apart in the Montague–Capulet

feud, and although there is an order-figure in the Prince, he
dominates the action only fitfully. Troilus is caught in the
war between Greeks and Trojans, and Antony between the
Roman and Egyptian worlds. In such a situation, personal
loyalty is likely to be deflected from society and to concentrate
on sexual love or family loyalties. These three plays, in particular, are tragedies of love or passion, and they are Shakespeare's version of the tragedy of the son, the crushing out of
vitality in a world where two social powers grind on each
other. This vitality is Dionysian, the energy of physical nature,
but because it is crushed, the hero resembles Dionysus rather
in his role as a dying or suffering god. Romeo's story follows
the general outline of the various dying-god stories available
to Shakespeare, in Ovid and elsewhere, the closest analogue
being that of Pyramus. Troilus does not die in his play, but
his role is similar dramatically. Antony is not young, but his
tremendous physical vitality makes him the most Dionysian
of the three—in fact Plutarch calls him the new Bacchus.
Sacrificial imagery may occur anywhere in a Shakespearean
tragedy, but when the context is the tragedy of order it is
usually more closely related to the analogy between the individual and the social body. An example is Marcus' speech in
Titus Andronicus:

> O let me teach you how to knit again
> This scattered corn into one mutual sheaf,
> These broken limbs again into one body.

Dionysus and the other gods of the cycle of life and death
in nature are, in the earlier forms of the myth, closely associated with a female figure who represents the basis of that
cycle, or Mother Earth. The god becomes the lover of the

goddess, is cast off or sacrificed, and dies; the goddess does not die. The god is subordinated to her, and in her relation to him she is sinister or treacherous as well as loving. This relationship survives in the courtly love poetry of Elizabethan lyrics, where the mistress is coy, cruel, or in extreme cases brings about her lover's death or madness and gloats over her achievement.

The women loved in the passion-tragedies have all the "white goddess" characteristics of someone whom it is death to love. Cleopatra is the tantalizing mistress, Cressida the treacherous siren, whose infidelity repeats and reverses the original action of Helen, thereby making the latter a part of the turning wheel of history, and Juliet is the bride in the midst of enemies. All of these, like the Duchess of Malfi, assume the ancient female prerogative of choosing their own lover, and are abused or despised in consequence by the male-dominated societies they belong to. Cressida is the archetype of falsehood; Cleopatra, to the Romans, is whore and gipsy; Juliet's father puts on quite a *senex iratus* show without even knowing the real facts of her situation. Something of the elusiveness of these figures comes into the raising of them to the upper stage—Juliet on the balcony, Cleopatra on the monument, Cressida on the walls of Troy—which is a recurrent feature of this group of plays.

The tragedy of love is the tragedy of Eros, a name which turns up in a significant context in *Antony and Cleopatra*, and Eros is also subordinated to his mother Venus. The maternal phase of the white-goddess cycle is represented by the ferocious mother of Coriolanus, Volumnia, whose supreme happiness as a mother consists not so much in giving her son life as in exposing him to death. Here again the social order is split into something very like a civil war of patricians and plebeians, and the crisis of the action of *Coriolanus* is, as in the other passion-tragedies, a collision of personal and social loyalties. Again, we have suggested a parallel between the victim of the passion-tragedy and the rebel of the order-tragedy, and the wives of the rebel-figures sometimes show a similar parallel with the passion-heroines. Gertrude is less aware of what she is doing than Cressida, but her dramatic function is like Cressida's in slipping so promptly from Hamlet's father to his enemy. Lady Macbeth is a less morally acceptable encouragement to her husband than Volumnia to her son, but the dramatic roles are analogous.

A tragic hero may be an older man or a younger man, a paternal or a filial figure: the tragedy of order is the typical Shakespearean form of the fall of the older man, and the tragedy of passion the typical Shakespearean form of the fall of the younger one. Both types of tragic hero may appear in the same play, in *Hamlet*, for example, where two fathers are killed and two sons also killed in efforts to avenge them. Ophelia's songs, which surely have as much to do with Hamlet's dead love as with "conceit upon her father," are concerned mainly with a Dionysus or Adonis figure ("you call him a-down-a," she says), a Prince Charming or bonny sweet Robin who comes to a maid on St. Valentine's day, who is borne on a bier and buried in a shroud white as "mountain snow," and whose death is full of the imagery of flowers and water, like the death of Ophelia herself. But in the final song the memory of Polonius is more obviously present: here the figure has a white beard as well as a flaxen poll, and the cycle is completed with the figure of the murdered father—the wheel becomes it, as she says. Ophelia is drowned, or drowns herself, while gathering flowers which are clearly phallic symbols, recalling a passage in Plutarch about the search of Isis for the body of Osiris.

Henry V is not a person that one would at first associate with the tragedy of passion, as he has probably less passion than any other major character in Shakespeare. But he is Shakespeare's most complete example of the cyclical movement of the youthful tragic hero, and so establishes the context for the group of passion-tragedies. Of the great conquerors of history, the most famous are Caesar and Alexander. Caesar had consolidated his power and was of mature years at the time of his death, hence his role in tragedy is that of an order-figure who has developed from the favourite of fortune into becoming part of the order of nature, and whose achievement becomes an even greater memory. Alexander died in youth, and his triumphs, dramatically speaking, instantly disappeared: he is the supreme example of the young hero raised by the wheel of fortune to its height and then thrown off. Henry is England's Alexander, the parallel being called to our attention by Fluellen. He starts in a Dionysian role of a wild madcap prince, with Falstaff his Silenus tutor, and the imagery associated with him is that of a midsummer night's dream. Falstaff speaks of their group as "Diana's foresters, gentlemen of the shade, minions of the moon," and Ely later remarks:

> And so the Prince obscured his contemplation
> Under the veil of wildness, which, no doubt,
> Grew like the summer grass, fastest by night.

And Falstaff's last words are "I shall be sent for soon at night." But although Falstaff's company "go by the moon and the seven stars, and not by Phoebus," the prince informs us that he is going to turn his back on this Dionysian role, "imitate the sun," and become something more like an incarnation of Apollo.

If we think of Henry simply as a hero of action, that is, if we take the point of view of the chorus, we shall see him as a prince of the most radiant and triumphant glory. Alexander was much preoccupied with his resemblance to divinity: Henry is not, but several touches in the imagery make him a preternatural figure, a Messiah treading the winepress. In Falstaff's company Henry takes on fallen human nature: as he says, in the regular imagery of night, "I am now of all humours that have showed themselves humours since the old days of goodman Adam to the pupil age of this present twelve o'clock at midnight." But when he becomes king, according to Canterbury, he becomes an unfallen Adam:

> Consideration like an angel came
> And whipped th' offending Adam out of him,
> Leaving his body as a paradise
> T' envelop and contain celestial spirits.

He describes a conspiracy against him, which we shall glance at again, in the familiar phrase "a second fall of man," and his conquest of France has apocalyptic overtones. France is twice called the "world's best garden," and its cities turn into a "maid," like the New Jerusalem.

But of course other things are going on too. There is a markedly disapproving emphasis on what amounts to the killing of Falstaff. Fluellen, not a person temperamentally much in sympathy with Falstaff, compares his death to Alexander's murder of Clitus, which, being done in hot blood, under great provocation, and bitterly repented afterward, brings out the coldness of Henry all the more clearly. There is the gradual disappearance of our other old friends, as Bardolph and Nym are hanged and the disgraced and beaten Pistol, his wife dead, goes back to a life of begging and stealing. In a tyranny, we said, there is often a sharp focus on a youthful victim: here, where the sense of tyranny is carefully muted and left only to implication, the Boy, whose shrewd comments make him a kind of infant Falstaff, simply vanishes, doubtless murdered by the enemy. The world's best garden, as Burgundy's speech shows, is a ruin, and Henry is appealed to to do something about it as soon as it is, as he says, "all mine." But, as we know, he dies at once; the war goes on and on, and the only result of his marriage to Katharine is Henry VI, the most pitiful creature in all Shakespeare. At the beginning of *Henry VI* La Pucelle says:

> With Henry's death the English circle ends:
> Dispersed are the glories it included.

And, however many fiends La Pucelle may keep company with, she is dead right. What we see in the play from this point of view is an illustration of the remark in the Epilogue: "Fortune made his sword." And Fortune, according to the useful Fluellen, is "painted also with a wheel, to signify to you, which is the moral of it, that she is turning, and inconstant, and mutability, and variation: and her foot, look you, is fixed upon a spherical stone, which rolls, and rolls, and rolls." Even at the beginning of the play we notice some oddly elegiac cadences. The sentimental Canterbury urges

Henry to revive the glory of Edward III's time, when the
chronicle of England was as full of praise

> As is the ooze and bottom of the sea
> With sunken wrack and sumless treasuries.

The play does not build up to an attitude that we are
expected to take, to a view that coincides with whatever
Shakespeare "had in mind." Shakespeare is neither the mouth-
piece of a jingoistic audience nor an over-subtle ironist. We
are quite free to admire Henry or to regard him as detestable.
There is plenty of textual evidence for both views, but neither
view of him will alter the structure of the history play he is
in. And what the structure of a history play says to us is:
"This is the essential poetic significance of something that
really happened." From the point of view of France, Henry
is a rebel-figure, a Tamburlaine or scourge of God who
explodes within a weak and demoralized social order and
destroys it in a tragedy of blood. In France, Henry is an
angel of death, which is what Coriolanus is also described
as being to the enemies of Rome, in one of those many passages where the echoes and overtones of a statement sound
very different from the context of the statement itself:

> He was a thing of blood, whose every motion
> Was timed with dying cries.

There is no incongruity, even from the French point of view,
in Henry's making such a to-do over the legitimacy of his
claim to the French throne when his claim to his own was
so doubtful. Henry is repeating the legend of his patron St.
George, coming over the sea and acquiring the country *de*

facto by conquest, and *de jure* by marrying the king's daughter. From the point of view of England, Henry's story is not a tragedy, because it ends in triumph and marriage. But it is one episode of what is, in its totality, a tragic vision, the cycle of nature and of fortune, of which the victims of the passion-tragedies represent other episodes.

In the tragedies of order, it is the function of the nemesis-figure to re-establish a disrupted continuity. The continuity is personal as well as social: Hamlet and Malcolm are the sons of the kings they avenge, and Octavius is a Caesar. In the tragedies of passion there is a conflict between personal and social loyalties. Henry V has no nemesis problem, but when his father dies, he makes the crucial social transition from prince to king, using "prince" here in the sense of heir apparent, someone who is still technically a private citizen, and who can therefore be presented dramatically in a "madcap" role without stirring up the anxieties of censorship. As king, he is confronted with two surviving father-figures. One, the Chief Justice, is the symbol of Henry's new social duties in his Apollo role of sun-king; the other, Falstaff, is the symbol of his old night-time companionship of tavern and highroad. Henry wipes Falstaff out of his life, hence, as it is somewhat disconcerting to observe, the role of the martyred father in *Henry V* is taken by Falstaff, not an order-figure but a disorder-figure, a lord of misrule. In destroying Falstaff, Henry also destroys, along with his sense of humour, an inner tension within society itself, the resistance to what Falstaff calls "old father antic the law." This inner tension explodes in a far more sinister form as soon as Henry dies, and becomes, so to speak, a nemesis of misrule. Falstaff's whole being is in his relation to Prince Henry—"Before I knew thee, Hal, I knew nothing," he says—and, as long as the Prince is a madcap, Falstaff is a parasite, a corrupt recruiting sergeant, and something of a brigand. As an attendant on a victorious king, he might well have settled into the role of professional jester, so important as a safety-valve in court life. He is given to drinking and wenching, but so are the jesters of the comedies. As it is, he has the role of rejected commentator on the action of *Henry V*, his place being taken by a properly disciplined chorus. For it is the function of the chorus in *Henry V*, as of Gower and Time in the romances, to put us into as uncritical a frame of mind as possible.

Henry's one passion is for conquest, and the conquest, as the cities are turned into a maid, takes the form of the play's heroine, the Princess Katharine. Setting the play in its historical context, the Princess, representing France as the object of fatal love, modulates into the sinister Queen Margaret of the earlier *Henry VI* plays, the source of so much disaster immediately after Henry's death. The theme of the fateful bride is thus present by implication in *Henry V* also.

Coriolanus is also related to the passion-tragedies, as already suggested. The three women of this play, Volumnia, Virgilia, Valeria, with their echoing names, seem at first to be merely the hazy "womenfolk" of a man's world. But very soon we are aware that Coriolanus is mother-dominated: even the crowd knows this, and remarks that he fights to please his mother. His sexual energy has gone into warfare, and his real mistress is Bellona, but though he is a leader in battle, there is a withdrawn and remote quality in him that has something adolescent about it. Other people are not quite real to him: he forgets the name of the Volscian who befriended him, and stands for consulship in a world of "voices." He fights so prodigiously that he is an army in himself, and when wronged he returns in irresistible strength, only the pleas of his mother and sweetheart being able to deflect his vengeance. His story, in short, is a boy's dream come true, and the complete solitude both of his assault on Corioli and of his exile (in Plutarch he has a band of followers on both occasions) emphasizes the dreamlike quality. Everybody calls Coriolanus proud, but that is not his trouble: his unwillingness to boast of his exploits and his horror of using them for political ends have much more to do with humility, in the most genuine sense. He has the charm, as well as the *gaucherie,* of a youth, the attractiveness of a man who cannot lie. But he has no power of holding a social order together: wherever he is, society seems to disintegrate. Even as an army leader, his soldiers follow him with enthusiasm only as long as things are going well: at the first check they break apart or fall to looting. The contrast with the soldiers of Antony, joking about their wounds even in the face of the most obvious disaster, is an instructive one.

Although a patrician, Coriolanus is not a conservative, in the good sense: one of his rare soliloquies speaks with contempt of tradition and custom. In standing for consul he is required to be, in our terms, an order-figure, but he cannot be anything more than a rebel-figure, a partisan of his own side. Shakespeare presents the social conflict in Rome through patrician eyes: the concrete details of the plebeians' grievances given by Plutarch are suppressed. Yet in being so favourable to the patricians, Shakespeare manages to bring out all the more clearly their alienation from the rest of Rome: they are so obviously an army of occupation that we feel little surprise at Coriolanus' going over to the Volscians without a twinge of conscience.

Volumnia has conditioned Coriolanus to feel that he must have an enemy: he loves his enemies in his own way, and if he loves anyone it is his enemy Tullus Aufidius. By making a friend of Tullus he becomes a predestined victim, and, during their quarrel, Tullus, with the cunning of a smaller man, calls him "boy." Coriolanus breaks down completely: it is, he says, the first time he is compelled to scold. It is also the first time he boasts, and he thereby exposes himself to being called a braggart. His collapse is the inevitable outcome of the scene in which his family, led by his mother, come to plead with him. Coriolanus in this scene is prepared for the assault on his feelings: what he does not know is that Volumnia is his superior officer, for it is only in his attitude to her that he recognizes authority. His cry of despair, "Oh, mother, what have you done?" accepts the fact that she is in effect condemning him to death, and links his story to the other tragedies of passion in which a woman's love is fatal.

The nearest thing to a father that Coriolanus has is Menenius Agrippa, who is a "humorous patrician," a strong partisan but a highly articulate one, and very useful to his own side because the citizens, even the tribunes, listen to him with a good deal of tolerance. He has a curious role, half counsellor and half jester, which reminds us in a very different way of Falstaff. The episode in which Menenius, confident of Coriolanus' love and full of paternal affection for him, comes to his tent and is brusquely dismissed is in some ways very like a minuscule version of the rejection of Falstaff, an annihilating snub which destroys his self-respect and even his reason for going on living.

In *Romeo and Juliet, Troilus and Cressida,* and *Antony and Cleopatra,* which are much more obviously tragedies of passion and fatal love, this counsellor-jester figure recurs, in Mercutio, in Pandarus, in Enobarbus. We notice that a set speech, usually calling attention to some central symbol of the play, is associated with the type. Menenius tells the fable of the belly and the members; Mercutio makes the Queen Mab speech; Enobarbus describes Cleopatra on her barge. Pandarus, being little more than an old fool, is hardly capable of a great speech of this kind, but the Falstaffian paternal, or avuncular, relation to the hero recurs in him, and his repudiation forms the bitter conclusion of a very bitter play. Mercutio and Enobarbus are not directly repudiated, but they are both destroyed by the colliding social forces of the plays they are in.

The Queen Mab speech becomes much more functional to *Romeo and Juliet* if we see the play in its context of passion-tragedies. The merest glance at the text will show how important the imagery of day and night, of light and darkness, is in it, and the play seems to be closely related, in its use of this imagery, to *A Midsummer Night's Dream,* which is probably near it in date. In the comedy there are two worlds: a day-world of Athens presided over by Theseus, full of bustle and hunting, and with laws to keep refractory lovers in order, and a night-world of a wood near Athens presided over by the fairies. This latter is a world of dreams and of sexual love, and its symbols are those of the cycle of nature, traditionally personified by the gods of love and of death, Eros and Adonis. Puck is an Eros figure squeezing the juice of a purple flower on sleeping lovers, and elsewhere in the wood Peter Quince's company is rehearsing a farcical version of the story of Pyramus, one of the many stories in which also, in the original Ovidian version, a purple or red flower springs from the dying hero's blood.

In the tragedy there is the day-world of Verona, when the Capulets are abroad and feuding is likely to break out, and the night-world of the Capulet party, the balcony scene, and the graveyard, where the sexual passion is fatal and ends in a much more serious version of the Pyramus story. The love itself is described as a day within a night, and, as in *A Midsummer Night's Dream*, the night-world is a Dionysian world:

> And fleckled darkness like a drunkard reels
> From forth day's path and Titan's fiery wheels.

And just as in the comedy the drive toward the fulfilment of love is carried through by the fairies and the tragic side of the story is reduced to parody, so in the tragedy the drive toward the fatal conclusion is in the foreground and the unseen impulses that prompt the lovers to fall in love so suddenly and so completely are suggested only by way of parody, in Mercutio's account of a fairy "hag" who evokes dreams of love from lovers. The sense of fatality and of a sinister sexual incubus (or succuba) is part of the character of Cressida and of Cleopatra: it is not part of the character of Juliet, and a special device is needed to suggest it. This is in spite of the fact that she rapidly bursts out of her role as a demure and bashful maiden at the Capulet party to become the Queen of the Night who calls to the horses of Phoebus to put an end to the day. Some curious phrases in the dialogue, such as "pink for flower," appear as jokes, going by too fast for us to see much significance in them.

The heroic society, most fully presented in the tragedy of order, is a society of action, and its two deadly rivals are feeling and thought. People who think too much, like Cassius, are dangerous to it: the isolating quality of thought and consciousness will be our next subject. But a continuous suspension of feeling is as necessary to the heroic life as a suspension of thought. A tragic action is *fully* tragic only to its spectators: heroes do not suffer except when they become objective to themselves. One great value of tragedy as a form of art is that it corrupts and weakens our heroism, refining our sensibilities by sapping our courage. It makes a fuss about murder and brutality, instead of accepting them as necessary pleasures of life. The tragedy of passion is in a peculiar sense the audience's tragedy: it is less spectacular than the tragedy of order, and is more intimate in its use of rhetoric.

In the tragedy of order the rhetoric of the controlling figures is of two kinds: the ruler's rhetoric and the counsellor's rhetoric. The counsellor's rhetoric consists mainly in building up a huge picture of society in which reality and appearance are presented as the same thing. Examples are Ulysses' speech on degree in *Troilus and Cressida*, designed to restore Achilles to his position of supremacy in the Greek camp, and the Archbishop of Canterbury's speech to Henry V comparing the state to a beehive, characterized by obedience, industry, consent, and an occasional massacre of drones. The ruler's rhetoric is at its clearest in the address to the army, as we have it in Henry V's exhortations before Harfleur and Agincourt and in the two harangues with which the action of *Richard III* goes into its last phase. Such rhetoric is hypnotic in its effect: there is usually a large element of lying in it, but it turns the wheel of the illusion of history, and the mob will not listen to anyone who, like Brutus or Coriolanus, disdains to use it. Brutus, like many liberals, is anti-rhetorical, and Coriolanus' "heart's his mouth": both are in consequence historical failures. It is essential to the purpose of such rhetoric that it should pretend not to be rhetoric: as with the counsellor's set speech, it presents its illusion as obvious reality. Thus Antony asserts that he is a plain blunt man, not an orator like Brutus, and Polonius, another counselling rhetorician, swears he uses no art at all.

The Dionysian heroes of the passion tragedies express themselves in a very different rhetoric from that of the king or counsellor, and, as elsewhere, there are instructive parallels in the histories. Hotspur is a vigorous and likeable figure, full of the natural vitality that in a disordered period is likely to become actively rebellious. The order-figure, we saw, is associated with music and with magic. Hotspur has a good deal of contempt for both music and poetry, the implication being that his destiny is not for kingship. He is also contemptuous of the occult: he lives in a bright daylight world a long way below the moon, and in that world Glendower's talk of magic and portents seems only neurotic obsession. Julius Caesar, however, was also a person of great common sense, but magic and portents surrounded him none the less. Thus Hotspur is a typical Dionysian figure of energy and fortune rather than of order and nature, a Phaethon, not the Phoebus that his rival Prince Henry is anxious to imitate. His rhetoric matches this impression: a remark made about it indicates that he might have been a greater man if he had been a duller one:

> He apprehends a world of figures here,
> But not the form of what he should intend.

Hotspur is at the opposite extreme from Richard II, whose rhetoric mirrors his fortunes: that is, it falls away from the situations he is in instead of battering against them. It is beautiful but self-indulgent, luxuriating in monologue but never consolidating a group. The quality of music and poetry in Richard's speech, the concentration on the pathos of his fall, and the touch of youthful narcissism about him, bring him much closer than any other of Shakespeare's kings to the victim-figures of the tragedies of passion. We notice that Richard seems deliberately to seek the kind of situation that calls for elegiac lament, and is recalled unwillingly from "that sweet way I was in to despair." It is right that he should be gazing at his reflexion in a mirror during the most public of his scenes, just as it is right for Henry V to describe himself as a person "that never looks in his glass for love of anything he sees there."

In the rhetoric of a breaking social order we hear fragments of the kind of oracular truth that according to Nietzsche is thrown up by the Dionysian elegiac lament in Greek tragedy. We hear them in Lear's maddened reflexions on justice, in Timon's misanthropy, in the cynicism of Enobarbus, in such comments as Williams' "there are few die well that die in a battle," just before the great gamble of Agincourt is risked and the horror of possible death is upon him. Such utterances are like sharp dissonances in classical music: however logical and right in their place, they are out of key with the whole design and have to be elaborately resolved within that design. Lear and Timon can be explained away as mad; Enobarbus is ultimately a creature of Antony; Williams is talked down by King Henry's sonorous monologue. And yet in these dissonances we hear what is described at the end of *King Lear* as one of the results of undergoing a tragic experience, when we are able to "Speak what we feel, not what we ought to say."

We have already noticed, particularly in the histories, how, although the order-figure has, *de jure,* the right to command, he seems to be able to escape final moral responsibility for the consequences of his commands. Henry IV condemns Exton as the murderer of Richard II even though he admits that Exton was carrying out his own wishes; Jack Cade is killed and sent to hell by Iden with great enthusiasm, though he is explicitly said to be a mere tool of the Duke of York. It is clear that the Eichmann plea, that we must do what we are ordered to do, belongs only to the purely ironic vision: it is not an integral part of the tragic vision, where there must be some power of self-determination for the least heroic character. Similarly, Henry V responds to Williams by a long prose speech explaining that although a king may command his soldiers to risk their lives, even to the point at which their death is practically certain, kings "purpose not their death when they purpose their services" and hence are absolved of responsibility for their deaths. One may understand the argument that a commander does not murder the soldiers killed under him, even if the commander is a king who has started the war essentially for kicks. But such a speech, delivered at such a place and time, and in disguise at that, has a quibbling and weaseling sound to it, and we may wonder what it is doing there.

It seems to me that it is serving a purpose in Shakespeare's histories rather similar, though a contrast, to the speech of God in Book Three of *Paradise Lost*. In Milton, God absolves himself of direct responsibility for Adam's fall, and, however unconvincing he may sound, Milton is trying through this speech to make God's will to redeem man seem more credible. In Shakespeare, Henry, by absolving himself of direct responsibility for the deaths of his soldiers, makes his proclamation ascribing the victory of Agincourt to God alone less hypocritical. What he is really saying is that he is not himself divine, for only a divine leader could assume the scapegoat role of responsibility. It was this aspect of the speech that commended it to Samuel Johnson, who always approved of speeches emphasizing human limitations. Brutus may be morally more attractive to us when he accepts responsibility for killing Caesar, but by doing so he limits his possible social function to that of a rebel-figure. The powers that be are ordained of God: the powers that be being what they are, this means that God ordains tragedy in human life, through the present constitution of nature.

The Trojan War, the theme of *Troilus and Cressida*, is, conventionally, the beginning of secular history, the convention being the assumption that the Trojans were the ancestors of the Romans and the Britons. The sense that the archetypes of history are being formed by the actions of the play is pervasive, and occasionally expressed: Pandarus says, for example, "let all pitiful goers-between be called to the world's end after my name; call them all Pandars; let all constant men be Troiluses, all false women Cressids." And because the side that attracts our sympathies is the losing side, the archetypes are those of the tragic vision. The Trojans are fighting to retain possession of Helen, to whom they have no moral right: this fact puts the Greeks into the nemesis-role that is usually victorious in tragedy. Yet we prefer Hector and Troilus: as in other tragedies of passion, it is the greater and more heroic vitality that is destroyed, something colder and meaner that succeeds with the Greek victory.

The two great tragic conceptions of being and time pervade the play: each is the subject of an eloquent speech by Ulysses. These two conceptions as presented are, respectively, the worlds of Tantalus and of Sisyphus. There is only a world of continuing process: nothing exists in the perfect tense, and nothing is ever really or permanently done. The greatest deeds of heroes must be continually repeated if the heroes are to be recognized. It is characteristic of this tragedy of passion that the order-figures, Priam and Agamemnon, should be in the background, subordinated both to the champions and to the counsellors. Achilles does come back, though only through the pure accident of the death of Patroclus, and he does vanquish Hector, though only by the kind of treacherous murder that anyone else could have encompassed equally well. So the wheel of fortune gets off to a good start. Things work out more or less as Ulysses had planned them, but not because he planned them: he is an instrument of fortune, but for all his wiliness he is Fortune's rejected counsellor, able to see her general design but not really able to direct it. His relation to

Achilles is parodied by Thersites' relation to Ajax, the latter all beef and no brains, the former too impotent to express his mental ability except in soliloquy or in the character of a "privileged man" or fool.

On the Trojan side, the Tantalus and Sisyphus themes are associated with the heroines, Helen and Cressida. The close linking of the heroic and the erotic is appropriate for a tragedy of this category, where heroism is seen as a deviation from love. Hector can see the absurdity of fighting for Helen, yet he allows himself to be over-ruled by Troilus' acceptance of the absurdity. Hector and Troilus agree to continue pushing the stone of "fame" and "glory" up the hill, though Hector at least clearly recognizes that it is a form of idolatry, a service of something that is not there. Troilus urges this course because of his love for Cressida, and Cressida wants an indefinitely prolonged Tantalus situation. She feels that she can only be adequately loved as long as she makes her lover "tarry," in the role of a perpetually elusive Courtly Love goddess. Once possessed by Troilus, an act she bitterly resents because it breaks her will to "hold off," she enters the world of Sisyphus, ready to be possessed again by whoever is present, like the host in Ulysses' time speech. She does not remain faithful to her original lover, but neither did Helen, who is Troilus's heroic inspiration.

Both Troilus and Cressida comment on the supremacy of the unconditioned will, and on the impossibility of keeping the will commanded by the reason, in love as in war. In the cosmos evoked by Ulysses' "degree" speech the reason does command the will, being its superior, but this order is not the order of history, in which the irrational plays so important a role. In a world where action and passion are the same thing, there can be no union of the reason and the will on equal terms. As actor, man is an impotent spectator; as spectator, an impotent actor. The latter role is represented in the kind of voyeurism which is senile in Pandarus and sardonic in Thersites; the former is in Ajax' lack of self-knowledge and Achilles' remark on his inability to see to the bottom of his own mind, as well as, on the Trojan side, in the failure of Hector and Troilus to understand the squalid malignancy of the way that things really happen.

The divided world of the passion-tragedies usually shows some correlation with another division between day and night, Apollo and Dionysus, common sense and romance, reality and desire, in which the Dionysian world is defeated. We saw something of this in the Henry IV plays and their alternation of dramatic interest between the historical theme, with Prince Henry as the emerging sun-king, and the night imagery attached to the Falstaff group. The same symbolic pattern is in *Romeo and Juliet*, with its subordinated "midsummer night's dream" theme, and even in *Coriolanus* there is a touch of a similar contrast between the plebeian daylight world of complaint and envy and the dreamlike world of the hero's exploits. The exploits make possible the kind of patrician life which produces Menenius, who describes himself as "one that converses more with the buttock of the night than with the forehead of the morning." *Troilus and Cressida* has no very prominent day and night pattern in its imagery, but it does contrast the Trojans, who are playing a romantic game, with the Greeks, who are simply out to destroy a city. One word frequently associated with Hector is "live": he dislikes killing people unless they are enemies of a type that fall within his strictly designed heroic code, and the contrast with Achilles, examining Hector and gloating with such pleasure over the idea of killing in itself, is a sharper form of the contrast between romantic and realistic worlds.

Both worlds are aspects of human nature, and both show human beings bound to acting out prescribed roles, rituals that they have created themselves. In the more romantic and idealistic world, the one that is destroyed by the tragedy, there is usually a greater sense of *gaya scienza*, a life with moments of passionate and profound joy. Defeated or not, we are never in any doubt about the reality of Romeo's love or Coriolanus' heroism. But in *Troilus and Cressida* there is a strong feeling of the quixotic and unreal quality of Trojan courtliness. The world that wins out in the comedies not only loses here, but has its values and standards called into question, an aspect of the play summed up in the repudiation of Pandarus, already mentioned. Hence *Troilus and Cressida* is not merely, so far as Hector is the hero, a tragedy; it is also, so far as Troilus is the hero, an anti-comedy. It therefore impresses us, in the age of the anti-hero, as a peculiarly modern play. But it will probably always seem a modern play, at least as long as the present age of irony lasts. The Trojans are not innocent in any intelligible sense of the word, but in Troilus' trust in Cressida and in Hector's chivalry there is a quality of innocence. The play dramatizes, not the loss of innocence, but the sense of the infinite vulnerability of innocence, however little of it there is and wherever it is, and the inevitability of the defeat of such innocence by experience. The two components of the tragic vision, the ironic sense of being in time and the heroic effort that struggles against it, are both very clearly presented, but the ironic vision, elaborated by Ulysses' two great speeches, is more dominant than in any other tragedy.

Antony and Cleopatra is the definitive tragedy of passion, and in it the ironic and heroic themes, the day world of history and the night world of passion, expand into natural forces of cosmological proportions. The Western and Roman world is pervaded by order, rule, and measure: when Antony tries to live by its standards he says:

> I have not kept my square; but that to come
> Shall all be done by th' rule.

Its commander is Octavius Caesar, the very incarnation of history and the world's greatest order-figure, a leader who is ruthless yet not really treacherous given the conditions of a ruler's task, who is always provided with all the justifications he needs for destroying Antony. Here, turning the wheel of history appears in its most persuasive form as conquering the world, and conquering the world, being thought of as ultimately the most real activity, is presented as a duty. It has many moral imperatives on its side, but we can hardly say that it is a pattern of virtue, at least so far as it affects Antony. As a Roman soldier, Antony reminds us more of the Antony in *Julius Caesar*, an altogether smaller character. His lieutenant Ventidius, in a highly significant speech, alludes to the danger of a subordinate's doing so well as to affect his superior's "image," as we would say now. Antony is much more calculating, when doing his conquering duty, than he is when he rewards the deserting Enobarbus, or when he turns the conference on Pompey's ship into an epiphany of Dionysus.

The Eastern and Egyptian world is presided over by Cleopatra, queen of the ancient and timeless land which renews its fertility by the overflowing of the Nile each year. The play opens with the remark that Antony's dotage "O'erflows the measure," which is a Roman view, and Cleopatra's world is a Dionysian world of gigantic feasting and drunkenness and love-making. Both worlds are equally hard on the taxpayer, to use a standard that Plutarch at least is aware of even if Shakespeare ignores it. Each world is a self-evident reality to itself and an illusion to its rival. To the Romans, Antony is "not Antony" in Egypt: to Cleopatra, if he stays there, he "will be himself." Antony himself, of course, tends to find his identity in his immediate context, and to waver disastrously between the two. But just as Octavius is the incarnation of history, so Cleopatra, like Falstaff, is a counter-historical figure. Most of what she substitutes for heroic action is idleness and distraction, and there is plenty of textual justification for making her a straight temptress like the other Renaissance sirens who entice the hero from his quest with some Bower of Bliss or lotus land. The Egypt of the play includes the Biblical Egypt, the land of bondage, and the Egypt of legend in which serpents and crocodiles are spawned from the mud of the Nile. Cleopatra, the serpent of the Nile, is a Venus rising from it in Enobarbus' speech; she wears the regalia of Isis; she is a *stella maris*, a goddess of the moon and the sea. She has affinities with the kind of goddess figure that both Hebraic and Classical religions kept trying to subdue by abuse: she is a whore and her children are all bastards; she is a snare to men and destroys their masculinity, making them degenerate slaves like Circe; she is an Omphale dressing her Hercules in women's clothes; she has many characteristics of her sister whore of Babylon. This last gives a curiously apocalyptic tone to the play: just as *Troilus and Cressida* is something of a secular fall, so *Antony and Cleopatra*, with its references to "Herod of Jewry," seems a kind of summing up of the old dispensation. The final cadences of the play seem to unite the two Biblical demonic themes, Egypt and the serpent, in a way that makes Cleopatra a central symbol of everything sinister in human history:

> This is an aspic's trail: and these fig-leaves
> Have slime upon them, such as the aspic leaves
> Upon the caves of Nile.

But *Antony and Cleopatra* is not a morality play, and Egypt is not hell: it is rather the night side of nature, passionate, cruel, superstitious, barbaric, dissolute, what you will, but not to be identified with its vices, any more than Rome can be identified with its virtues. Prince Henry finds himself in the same Dionysian night world when he is a youth, and still has the choice of going up the wheel of fortune and history or of plunging downward into a world which becomes with increasing clarity a world of thieves and whores. But Henry, like Odin in the Eddas, learns a good deal from his descent and escapes from it at the sacrifice of some of his humanity. Antony is on the other side of the wheel: he can only fall out of history and action into the anti-historical and mythical world of passion opposite it, where the dominating figure is female and the hero is her subordinate. The slighter and younger Octavius goes up the wheel and takes command of history: Antony goes on to a hero's destruction, yet even in his death he is upstaged by Cleopatra, who monopolizes the attention of the audience to the end, looking in her death ready to "catch another Antony" and start all over. She is worth the attention, because she is all we can see of a world as big as the Roman world, and not only all we can see of it but that world in herself, a microcosm of passion "whom everything becomes." Her Egypt is able to bring a superhuman vitality out of Antony that Rome cannot equal, not in spite of the fact that it destroys him, but because it destroys him.

At the close of the play the two ends of the wheel confront each other: the Cleopatra who has

> pursued conclusions infinite
> Of easy ways to die

and the Caesar who has been equally busy in pursuing difficult ways to live. Rome with its measure and order has won out over the overflowing Nile: the last line of the play urges us, in Caesar's voice, to see "High order in this great solemnity." But we can see something else besides high order: we see that there is a part of nature that can never be ordered, a colossal exuberance of powers, the tailors of the earth as Enobarbus calls them, that weave and unweave the forms of life. Antony has caught a glimpse of these powers at the price of disappearing like a cloud when "the rack dislimns," for it is only a self-destroying will that can bring one close to them. In fact Antony may say, with Slender in *The Merry Wives*, "I am freely dissolved, and dissolutely." Hercules has deserted him, but we remember how Hercules got rid of the burden of the world by tricking Atlas into re-assuming it: perhaps there is something gullible about Caesar, as Cleopatra suggests when she says she hears Antony

                              mock
         The luck of Caesar, which the gods give men
         To excuse their after wrath.

However, Caesar is now the master of his world, the secular counterpart to Christ, the off-stage presence in *Cymbeline* who is able to exact tribute from the end of the world in Britain even when defeated there. We say, in Roman terms, that Antony has lost "the world" for love. But his disappearance from that world is also, in a final twist of the tragic paradox, the appearance of another world that endures no master.

Little world
of man:
The tragedy
of isolation

Little world of man: The tragedy of isolation

In Shakespeare's tragedies certain moral issues are involved, and often, particularly in the histories and the Roman plays, our moral sympathies are divided. But in many of the greatest tragedies there is no division of moral sympathies at all. Whatever sympathy we may have for Iago, Edmund, Macbeth, or Claudius is dramatic, not moral. And yet the feeling of Shakespearean tragedy is authentic, in contrast to the less authentic version of tragedy that we call melodrama, where we feel impelled to applaud the hero and hiss the villain. *Titus Andronicus* seems to us less authentically tragic than *Hamlet*: the plot of *Hamlet* is slightly less violent, but not so much so as to make that the crucial difference. In authentic tragedy we participate in the action: we condemn Iago and Macbeth because they are what they are and yet have succeeded in making themselves extensions, for a moment, of ourselves. Melodrama leans to the moral and conceptual, and tries to identify us with a heroism we admire and separate us from a villainy we detest. Melodrama thus tends to find its emotional tragic focus in the punishment of the villain, and our reaction to that is primarily: "Oh, the difference from me!"

Thus melodrama appeals to emotions akin to those aroused in watching a public execution. The action of *The Spanish*

Tragedy is watched by a personified Revenge and the ghost of Don Andrea, a former lover of the heroine, Bel-imperia. Bel-imperia is in love with someone else when the play begins, and one wonders if the reason for Don Andrea's pleasure in the action is resentment that everybody has so completely forgotten about him. But no: the reason is that he just likes to see bloody things happening:

> Horatio murdered in his father's bower;
> Vile Serberine by Pedringano slain;
> False Pedringano hanged by quaint device;
> Fair Isabella by herself misdone;
> Prince Balthazar by Bel-imperia stabbed;
> The Duke of Castile and his wicked son
> Both done to death by old Hieronimo;
> My Bel-imperia fallen as Dido fell,
> And good Hieronimo slain by himself:
> Aye, these were spectacles to please my soul!

Occasionally we feel that a tragedy has manipulated its action in the direction of horror, just as a comedy may manipulate its action in the direction of a happy ending. The Cardinal, in Shirley's play of that name, is an unattractive but well-realized character for four acts, but when he goes on into attempted rape and poisoning we feel that the integrity of his character has been sacrificed to a blood-and-thunder conclusion. Such manipulation is melodramatic rather than tragic. Again, at the end of *Titus Andronicus* Aaron's fate is carefully spelled out for us: he is to be buried up to his waist in earth until he starves to death. His response to this is most satisfactory: a regret that he had not done ten thousand more evil deeds. The conclusion is tragically less authentic than the threat to torture Iago to death at the end of *Othello*, because, coming where it does in that play, it is the utter futility of revenge on Iago that most impresses us. Terrible things happen in Shakespeare's mature tragedies, but they do not happen with the particular kind of sadistic brutality that goes with appealing to high moral principles in the audience. In Ford's *'Tis Pity She's a Whore* the theme is brother-sister incest, and the sister's nurse, a harmless and amiable old woman who has connived at the incest, first has her eyes put out and then, as an act of justice applauded by the whole cast, is sentenced to be burned alive. This is the kind of audience response condemned by Blake when he remarks how, at a tragic scene, "The soul drinks murder and revenge and applauds its own holiness."

The Christian religion appears explicitly in Elizabethan tragedy mainly in connection with its doctrine of hell, and so usually has the same brutalizing and debasing effect as the morality which it reinforces. Hamlet's speech on Claudius' prayer belongs to the very common tragic convention of making sure that the villain dies at the time most inconvenient for his entry into the next world. The convention illustrates the difficulty that tragedy, which deals with the inescapable human situation, has with a God for whom all things ought to be possible. We saw that the Greek gods enforce the mortality of man: similarly the Christian God, in a Christian tragedy, is normally a *deus in machina*, stuck in a legal and sacramental machine, automatically sending Claudius to hell if he dies drunk, and to purgatory if he dies praying. In other words, God in tragedy is seen through a haze of human passion, and is created in the image of that passion. We have glanced already at the fact that God's main interest, in Elizabethan tragedy, is in promoting the revenge, and in making it as bloody as possible. The source of Middleton's *The Changeling* is a book called *The Triumphs of God's Revenge Against Murder*, though Middleton is more restrained than Ford and Tourneur, who are particularly fond of putting up signs reading "Danger—God at work" in the course of the action. In the Ford play just referred to, one character comments:

> I need not now—my heart persuades me so—
> To further his confusion; there is One
> Above begins to work: for, as I hear,
> Debates already 'twixt his wife and him
> Thicken and run to head.

In both of Tourneur's plays there is a muttering roll of thunder when the villainy has really gone too far. The religious dimension, in both Ford and Tourneur, goes with a moral interest that leads them to call their characters by allegorical names, like the Lussurioso and Ambitioso of *The Revenger's Tragedy*.

Christianity is—or was—a moral and conceptual system including a theme of salvation which is comic in shape, and a theme of damnation which is sub-tragic. Its climax, in which life is separated into a heaven and a hell where infinite torments are exacted for finite offences, is an apotheosis of melodrama. The existential form of tragedy has to wriggle out, as best it can, from underneath a religious doctrine where "grace and vengeance strangely join," as Isaac Watts puts it.

There is a Biblical injunction, "Vengeance is mine," but the vengeance of God being apparently of the same kind as the vengeance of cruel and malicious human beings, it is not difficult for any revenger to think of himself as the appointed instrument of divine wrath. The Hieronimo of *The Spanish Tragedy,* who quotes the passage, is one of many examples. When one reads Dante's *Inferno* one may reflect what an immense debt humanity owes to the people of Dante's day who placidly went on sinning, and thereby reached in experience some sense of the unreality of the conceptual nightmare. Among other things, they have forced us to read the poem less melodramatically, which in this case means less literally. *Faustus* is the great religious tragedy of false wisdom, as Tirso de Molina's Don Juan play is the great religious tragedy of false love. Both plays take their heroes to hell; both were in consequence very popular, and it is significant that both eventually became something of a circus. That is, the religious theme strongly suggested to their audiences unauthentic ways of responding to them.

There is, however, another conception of hell which is more genuinely tragic. Tragedy is concentrated on death as the essential event of life, and as far as the tragic action is concerned it is also the end of life. One much-abused female in Euripides remarks how horrifying it would be if death were *not* the end of life. We notice the extraordinary power, in Greek tragedy, of the desire to have one's body buried, planted in a definite spot and marked. The unburied body, "a prey to dogs and birds," in the Homeric phrase, is left to dissolve in the flux of time; burial is, at least symbolically, real death, or deliverance from time. This dimension of the theme comes unobtrusively but palpably into *Antigone*. But of course there was still a shade that survived in the world below, and this shade still felt all the tragic emotions of enmity and revenge. The ghost of Achilles demanded sacrifices; the ghost of Darius returned with sombre warnings for his successor. In the convention of the returning ghost, tragedy expresses something that does not in itself depend on any belief in survival after death. No event in time ever completes itself; no act of aggression fails to provoke revenge; no act of revenge fails to provoke another act of revenge. We have noticed how closely Shakespearean tragedy is linked to history, and history to the sense of the same kind of event going on without cessation. Hell, seen from this point of view, is an allegory of the unending torment of the human condition. As Thomas Dekker says: "There is a Hell named in our Creed, and a Heaven, and the Hell comes before; if we look not into the first, we shall never live in the last." A sour remark of one of Timon's servants indicates even more clearly that the real hell is the one we ourselves create: "The devil knew not what he did when he made man politic: he crossed himself by 't; and I cannot think but in the end the villainies of man will set him clear."

At the bottom of Dante's hell we find a three-headed Satan meditatively chewing Judas Iscariot, Brutus, and Cassius, one in each mouth. Judas we can understand, and we know something of Dante's secular anxieties from the *De Monarchia*. But Caesar is nobody in particular in the *Commedia*, merely a name in the upper regions of hell. Why should Brutus and Cassius be assigned the ultimate indignity of becoming two-thirds of the devil's bubble-gum? There are degrees of villainy in the *Inferno,* and apparently the traitor is to be considered the most detestable of all villains, whatever the motives for his treachery. There are implications here for the theory of tragedy that are of central importance.

We said that it is natural to man to be in a state of social discipline, hence the figure we called the order-figure, Caesar or Duncan or Agamemnon, represents the reality of human life, of being in time. And yet the more closely we examined this reality, the more it began to look like illusion as well. The order-figure, we saw, is an actor, wholly absorbed in appearance, and the wheel of history he turns is based on a constant round of battles. Battles are very serious matters to ordinary people, the non-heroic who are not allowed to wear heavy armour. One thinks of Falstaff's remark: "There's not three of my hundred and fifty left alive; and they are for the town's end, to beg during life." But to heroes battles are a game. It is not that they are never hurt or killed, but that battles for them are primarily a risking of or gambling with life, a game played with death as the stakes. Man is *homo ludens,* a player of games, and he is never more deeply engaged in play than when he is trying to kill someone at the risk of being killed himself.

The coward is despised because he refuses to play the game, and so reminds us that it is a game, and that we have a choice of not playing it. In the "ecstatic" heroic society one's life is in one's loyalties: to die bravely in battle is still, in a very real sense, to preserve one's essential life. The coward feels that the centre of life is not in his leader or society but in himself. He is feared as well as despised, because unless his behaviour is shouted down with contempt and ridicule there will be a slight suggestion about it of sanity in the midst of hysteria. This suggestion is tolerable only when released as humour, as it is in Falstaff's speeches on honour and counterfeits. Falstaff in these speeches is not so much a clown as the spokesman of the ironic vision that outlives the tragic one.

The hypocrite is another character type who is isolated from the tragic society. There is an etymological connexion between the hypocrite and the masked actor. In a sense we are all hypocrites because we all wear social masks or personae, as Timon says to the painter, referring to the fall of man:

> The painting is almost the natural man;
> For since dishonour traffics with man's nature,
> He is but outside.

The strong man or successful ruler is the man who is no longer aware of a disparity between reality and appearance, and is able to live in a continuous state of self-hypnosis. There is something to be said for genuine hypocrisy, if the phrase is not an oxymoron: to be constantly aware of an incongruity between what one says and what one is takes a degree of skill, self-discipline, even honesty, of a type that one would hardly expect from a mere vice. After three plays in which a long procession of characters move in and out like figures in a waving tapestry, Richard III hits us with the impact of complete humanity, assuming that great wickedness is a necessary part of that completeness. This is because he is a hypocrite, an actor who knows he is putting on a show, and he establishes a dramatic bond with us in spite of ourselves, as though he were giving us a confidential wink. Richard is naturally less likeable than Falstaff, but he has something of Falstaff's capacity to attach himself to the audience even as he loses contact with his own society. The ghosts who appear to him at Bosworth suggest to us that in proportion as one conceals oneself from the tragic society one makes oneself visible to the unseen world of the dead, from which revenge so frequently comes. Richard divides the sympathies of the audience in the same way that he divides his own mind. Our attention is turned toward the play, where Richard is a lively, even an exhilarating, source of dramatic action, but we have deep moral reservations about what he is doing that identify with the ghosts of death and revenge.

The traitor is much more disturbing than the coward or hypocrite. It is the first postulate of the heroic society that no traitor can be honourably motivated: no enemy's cause is just, because justice cannot exist apart from loyalty to one's own leader. The coward goes on living in his society, however shamed and disgraced; the traitor suggests the nothingness, the sense of annihilation, inherent in the dissolving of the social group. This nothingness or not-being is an abyss far deeper than death, for death in itself affects only the individual, and the individual is not, in this conception, the ultimate form of human life. Hence though the coward and hypocrite may speak directly to us, with the oracular ring of unacceptable truth in what they say, the traitor remains more inscrutable. His motto is Iago's "Demand me nothing: what you know, you know." We recognize this inscrutability even in Iago's soliloquies: when he says

> For that I do suspect the lusty Moor
> Hath leaped into my seat: the thought whereof
> Doth like a poisonous mineral gnaw my inwards

he is not really trying to rationalize his own villainy, and so taking us into his confidence: he is merely trying to poison our minds against Othello.

There are two levels of treason: the lower one is betrayal of one's society to an enemy society; above it comes conspiracy, or a purely internal rebellion against the ruler. This latter, besides being the central theme of the order-tragedies, is deeply ambiguous. Brutus and Cassius in Shakespeare are certainly not the simple traitors that they are in Dante. From his own point of view, Brutus is not a rebel but, as Beddoes calls him, the saint of avengers, and Caesar to him represents not an object of loyalty but a menace to loyalty. We remember the couplet:

> Treason never doth prosper. What's the reason?
> Why, if it doth prosper, none dare call it treason.

There is a sense, and a not particularly cynical sense, in which this is true. If Brutus had been more like Antony, more ruthless, self-centred, and realistic, his relation to Caesar would have been much more like Caesar's relation to Pompey. Bolingbroke, again, was not a traitor, because he won, but if Richard II had been a stronger ruler he would certainly have died a traitor's death.

Bolingbroke's son Henry V *is* a strong ruler, and when the Cambridge-Scroop-Grey conspiracy against him fails the horrified king remarks:

> I will weep for thee;
> For this revolt of thine, methinks, is like
> Another fall of man.

The phrase is echoed from the garden scene in *Richard II*, and indicates that Henry V has, for the moment, put an end to the cycle of disorder that began with the deposition of Richard, and has finally crushed the cause of the Earl of Mortimer, who *de jure* had a better claim to the throne than he had, as we are reminded in *Henry VI*. These conspirators are traitors in the lower sense of being willing to betray their country to France, and Henry at the time is deeply sunk in what we have called the self-hypnosis of a successful ruler about to start a major war. His father, just before his death, had pointed out to him that the most effective way of dealing with rebellious temperaments was to keep them busy with "foreign quarrels." But even so the remark gives us an important clue to the meaning of treason in Shakespeare. The traitor reminds us of what the doctrine of original sin reminds us, that human life is an ironic condition, and that the greatest efforts of loyalty and heroism can raise it only from the ironic into the tragic. And if the human condition can be seen as unendingly ironic or tragic, it is being seen as life in hell, with the traitor closest to the source of personal evil.

In melodrama the effort is to separate the audience from the villain: melodrama speaks comfortable words, like "hanging is too good for him." It seeks to persuade the audience that they are a part of a social order more reassuring than the ironic or the tragic. We notice that the three conspirators against Henry V all make speeches in turn explaining how glad they are to be caught and punished. It is clear that the phenomenon now known as brain-washing is not the invention of this politically very unoriginal age. There is some suggestion of being relieved from a kind of demonic possession, of a type that seems to run through history with its own version of *de jure* succession. We find this again in the death of the Thane of Cawdor in *Macbeth*, where there is also a suggestion that the demonic possession passes from the old Thane of Cawdor into the new one: Malcolm, in his turn, seems aware of the danger of inheriting it from Macbeth. More important is the fact that such repentant traitors are seeking the consolations of melodrama for themselves. They are referred to in Sonnet 124 as "fools of time"

> Which die for goodness, who have lived for crime.

The word "fool" in Shakespeare, when used in direct connection with time, nature, or fortune (as in Romeo's phrase "fortune's fool" and Lear's "the natural fool of fortune"), means essentially the person to whom things happen, the one who cannot control events. The successful ruler is a combination of nature and fortune, *de jure* and *de facto* power. He steers his course by the tiller of an immediate past and by the stars of an immediate future. He is resolute and decisive, and yet his actions in a way rest on a continuous suspension of decision, for he acts as an agent or instrument for the decisions of nature. Antony finds that Octavius has better luck at games than he has: the significance of this is not simply that Octavius' fortune is in the ascendant, but that his fortune is better synchronized with the natural course of events. It is this synchronizing of nature and fortune that soothsayers study, and that the witches in *Macbeth* know something about. We call it fate, which over-simplifies it. The soothsayer in *Antony and Cleopatra* calls it, more accurately, "nature's infinite book of secrecy."

One feature of this "fate" is the sense of continuity in time, the preserving of which is what makes legitimacy so important a principle of government. The order-figure experiences time as the rhythm of his actions. He does things when it is time to do them, and the sense of responding to the moment gives a continuous dramatic exhilaration to his life. Julius Caesar is almost devoid of anything that we should call anxiety: death "will come when it will come," and he can hardly understand any other attitude. In the pre-tragic first act of *Othello*, Othello tells Desdemona that she will have to fit into his busy schedules as best she can, because "we must obey the time." Prince Henry uses the New Testament phrase "redeeming time" about his proposed emergence from the world of Falstaff into the world of action, and later, Exeter, explaining to the King of France that Henry V is no longer a dissolute prince but an irresistible conqueror, says:

> Now he weighs time
> Even to the utmost grain.

The tragic rebel has committed himself primarily to fortune, and in fortune what happens depends on resolution, decision, and will, instead of on a natural course of events to be followed. Hence, as soon as the rebel-figure plans his rebellion, he has a sense of having broken through the continuity of time. He no longer has any sense of the present moment: he is conscious only of the "gap of time" that Leontes falls into when he becomes jealous. We recall the famous speech of Brutus:

Between the acting of a dreadful thing
And the first motion, all the interim is
Like a phantasma or a hideous dream.
The Genius and the Mortal instruments
Are then in council, and the state of man,
Like to a little kingdom, suffers then
The nature of an insurrection.

The last word draws attention to the identity of Brutus' inner mental state and his political situation. He is now in a state of "dread": everything is thrown forward to a future moment, and that moment, when reached, will become an irrevocable past. The future moment is the moment of guilt, and it imposes on one, until it is reached, the intolerable strain of remaining innocent. As Atreus says in Seneca, once he has determined on cooking his brother's children for his brother's dinner: "Why do I remain innocent so long?" We notice that anyone who is forced to brood on the past and expect the future lives in a world where that which is not present is present, in other words in a world of hallucination. Macbeth's capacity for seeing things that may or may not be there is almost limitless, and the appearance of the mousetrap play to Claudius, though more easily explained, has the same dramatic point as the appearance of Banquo's ghost. Brutus speaks of a "hideous dream" with the Genius in council; the assassination summons up an evil genius in the form of Caesar's ghost. The fact that murder is a uniquely *uncanny* crime has a good deal to do with the sense of breaking the temporal continuity of existence.

Of course the moment of guilt is also the moment of opportunity, the catching of the tide in the affairs of men. But the rebel, as a rule, is not the instrument of nature, whose rhythms, if often destructive and terrible, are always leisurely. He himself is the source of decision, and so the sooner he acts on his decision the better. Satan remarks to Christ in *Paradise Regained*:

> Each act is rightliest done
> Not when it must, but when it may be best.

and Christ himself said to his betrayer: "What thou dost, do quickly." The resolute or autonomous decision, then, is always hurried: it violates time, just as the violent death is untimely (or, in Elizabethan language, "timeless"). Brutus, as soon as he has got his army into a strong position, cannot endure the strain of waiting, and makes a resolute decision to take it out to Philippi, where it is cut to pieces. When Claudius marries Gertrude, Hamlet is more outraged by the "wicked speed" of the event than by the "incestuous" aspect of it, and Claudius' later hurry in getting Polonius buried "in hugger-mugger" indicates his demoralization. That Macbeth is being hurried into a premature act by his wife is a point unlikely to escape the most listless member of the audience, but Macbeth comes to regret the instant of fatal delay in murdering Macduff, and draws the moral that

> The flighty purpose never is o'ertook
> Unless the deed go with it. From this moment
> The very firstlings of my heart shall be
> The firstlings of my hand.

That is, in future he will try to attain the successful ruler's spontaneous rhythm of action. Even in the more domestic and

mercantile setting of the fall of Timon, we can still hear the
theme of the breaking of time in the steward's speech:

> 'Tis all engaged, some forfeited and gone,
> And what remains will hardly stop the mouth
> Of present dues. The future comes apace.
> What shall defend the interim?

The same feeling of broken rhythm comes into the passion-
tragedies too, especially *Romeo and Juliet*. The sense of a love
that is "too rash, too unadvised, too sudden," of something
that explodes and hurls its victims to destruction (the image
of gunpowder is frequently used), hangs over the whole play,
and is expressed not only by such agents of professional
caution as Friar Laurence, but by the lovers themselves.

The ideal source of the rhythm of time which the successful
ruler accommodates to human action is indicated in Henry
VI's pathetic speech expressing his own longing to retreat from
the world of rule and rebellion to a pastoral world where time
is experienced as a pure becoming, where such a phrase as
"ripeness is all" has its real meaning and is not merely a
command to live out the whole of a miserable life:

> To carve out dials quaintly, point by point,
> Thereby to see the minutes how they run,
> How many makes the hour full complete;
> How many hours brings about the day;
> How many days will finish up the year;
> How many years a mortal man may live.
> When this is known, then to divide the times.

The link is obvious and significant with the colloquy between
Touchstone and Jaques in *As You Like It*, and indicates how

the pastoral and the recovery of time are both symbols of a higher level of nature than history as such can reach, even though the social discipline of war brings us closer to it than the lack of discipline which is what is so often meant by peace. At the opposite extreme is Macbeth's "tomorrow" speech, where the experience of time is the demonic parody of Henry's.

Of the three great rebel-figures, Claudius, morally, is half-way between the "noblest Roman" Brutus and the "butcher" Macbeth. He has committed a detestable crime, but still he is a born ruler, prompt in danger, affable and gracious in peace, and an affectionate husband. For the early part of the play, at least, he seems genuinely attached to Hamlet. Hamlet's view of him is a natural one for Hamlet to take, but is not always consistent with the impression Claudius himself gives. Claudius also delays in striking down Hamlet, and also gives unconvincing excuses for his delay. The main structure of the play is the one we have mentioned, with Claudius the usurper and Hamlet the avenger; but on this is superimposed a secondary pattern. Claudius is a real king, with some divinity hedging him; Hamlet is not sure that the ghost is authentic, and then he himself, through his blunder in killing Polonius, stirs up his own nemesis in Laertes. Hence Hamlet has some of the rebel-figure's characteristics, especially the feeling that the time is out of joint and the necessity of forcing himself into resolute decisions. Hamlet, however, is primarily a nemesis-figure, an avenger who is in the position of trying to achieve some identity, both individual and social, by a destructive act. And just as the act of seizing power is subject to hurry, so the act of vengeance is subject to delay. If the vengeance is just, it represents a reintegrating of nature and fortune, and so has to wait for the natural course of events. As Hieronimo says in *The Spanish Tragedy*:

> Wise men will take their opportunity,
> Closely and safely fitting things to time.
> But in extremes advantage hath no time;
> And therefore all times fit not for revenge.

If God is on the side of the vengeance, the avenger must wait for God's time, which is usually very slow for human impatience. Thus Charlemont, the pious hero of *The Atheist's Tragedy*, is led to the very brink of death before events work out in his favour.

The avenger reintegrates time by starting a new cycle, whatever the moral status of his revenge. Even the abortive attempt at revenge on Claudius by Laertes is hailed by the crowd "as the world were now but to begin." Like the rebel-figure, the nemesis-figure may be of any moral status. Antony in *Julius Caesar*, with his unscrupulous rhetorical tricks, his cynical use of Caesar's will, and his determination to treat Lepidus as a "property," is not a very attractive figure, but the irresistible power of a new cycle of time is on his side. Cassius almost kills himself in obedience to this principle of a renewed cycle: the battle of Philippi is fought on his birthday and so "time is come round." Edmund's "wheel is come full circle" is another reluctant tribute of rebellion to its returning adversary. This theme is at its clearest where we are most in sympathy with the nemesis. Thus at the end of *Macbeth*, after the proclamation "the time is free," and of promises to make reparations of Macbeth's tyranny "Which would be planted newly with the time," there will be a renewal not only of time but of the whole rhythm of nature symbolized by the word "measure," which includes both the music of the spheres and the dispensing of human justice, the opposite of Richard II's anarchy where "time is broke and no proportion kept."

We notice how frequently the avenger has to be completely isolated from the action, generally by exile, before the nemesis can take place. Bolingbroke and Richmond come from overseas; Malcolm and Macduff from England; Hamlet, like so many heroes of folk tales, lands "naked" on Danish shores; Edgar emerges from his Poor Tom role and Cordelia, in an effort at nemesis that fails, invades England from France; Coriolanus, Lucius, and Alcibiades in *Timon* come back in vengeance to their native cities. Avengers are to be distinguished from traitors, and obviously they are never cowards; but they are usually isolated from a tragic society in a similar way: they have to *face* the action, so to speak, before being reintegrated with it.

We may now apply our principles of isolation to the three-fold structure of the tragedy of order. We have the parody of the order-figure in the tyrant, who, like Richard III or Macbeth, is the leader of his society but is not attached to it. What the tyrant does he does primarily for self-interest, and hence he tends as he goes on to become more and more incapable of anything except murder. The traitor, like Iago or Edmund, is a parody of the rebel-figure, whose actions dissolve and disintegrate his society: naturally he is identical with certain types of rebel-figure, such as Macbeth. Third, we have certain characters isolated by the action of the play, like Lear or Timon, who become parodies of a nemesis-figure, making futile threats of revenge. Othello, with his talk of "the cause" and of "sacrifice," is also a nemesis parody. The tyrant and traitor increase the evil of the world they are in, but they desert the order of nature for the wheel of fortune. Hence, while their regimes are worse than those of their predecessors, they are also less inevitable, as they give the wheel of fortune a harder push that will eventually bring them down and their nemesis up. This process gives us a normal and morally intelligible tragic action ending in the post-tragic contract already discussed.

These three types tend to be attracted to two opposite poles. At one pole is the character who is involved wholly in, and seems to enjoy, the tragic action he brings about, whether he is a tyrant like Richard III or a traitor like Iago and Edmund. He could also be a nemesis-figure, though there is no example in Shakespeare, except for a few moods of Hamlet: a more typical example is Tourneur's Vendice, who surrenders himself to justice as soon as he has established the justice. Such a character is for a time a demonic parody of the successful ruler: Iago, in particular, seems to create the tragedy of Othello with a successful ruler's sense of timing. This type also has about him some feeling of a master of ceremonies or lord of misrule, a perverted artist in crime, a sinister Prospero evoking his own drama, even a kind of macabre clown. The connexion of this last with Richard III is clear enough, and still clearer in Marlowe's Barabas. These "Machiavellian" characters are projections of the author's will to direct the action to a tragic end: they fascinate us and inspire a reluctant admiration, but they are always set over against us.

At the other pole is the character whose isolation from the

action has intensified his consciousness. He has withdrawn from the social group and is now seeing it as objective, as facing him with indifference or hostility. But he is seeing it, so to speak, from our own side of the stage, and his thoughts are for the moment ours. Most of the really titanic figures of Shakespearean tragedy are in this position for most of the play, Lear, Othello, Hamlet, and Macbeth included, and it is the presence of this perspective that makes the tragedy authentic. These two poles of dramatic interest are not the moral poles, the simple difference between the right side and the wrong side. The dramatic and the moral placing of characters syncopate against each other, creating a complex pattern of sympathies without confusing us about our ultimate reactions.

"I am myself alone," says Richard III: he is not at all a coward and the term traitor is too simple for him, but his relation to his society eventually becomes unreal. To understand this fully we have to see him in his context, as the end of a long process of social disintegration which has gone on all through the vast tetralogy that ends with his death. We mentioned Talbot, the hero of the first part of *Henry VI*, and his remark to the French countess who tries to take him prisoner that he is his own shadow, his substance being in his followers. Talbot's chief opponent is La Pucelle, better known as Joan of Arc. La Pucelle in *Henry VI* is so complex a character that some critics ascribe her to two authors, the one they approve of being Shakespeare. She speaks eloquently of her mission and of France's case (her rhetoric is supposed to hypnotize Burgundy at once); she seems genuinely possessed by a belief in her own purity and nobility of descent, and may have turned to her "fiends" in an act of genuine patriotism.

She has a brusque realism and, though terrified of death for herself, she has an accurate sense of the rise and fall of fortune in history. No actress could bring unity out of the role, because the inter-connecting lines have not been written, and if they had been they would have shattered the framework of the play.

What Shakespeare is interested in is not La Pucelle's character, much less her cause, but the symbolism of two kinds of society. On the one side is the heroic, "ecstatic" society of Talbot, desperate and beleaguered; on the other is its opposite, a society created out of the ambition of one person. Help comes too late to save Talbot, but La Pucelle's victories are won with great speed, her promises, as King Charles says, bearing fruit instantly, like Adonis's gardens. The "fiends" appearing to her symbolize her type of society, and the contrast is essentially the same as that between the heroic but hard-pressed Duncan and the world of tyranny, treachery, witch-craft, illusion, and looking into the seeds of time set up by Macbeth. There is a suggestion that the instant La Pucelle is executed something of her spirit passes into Margaret, and thereby becomes imported into England. The first part con-cludes with an ironical comparison of the taking of Margaret to England with the carrying of Helen off to Troy by Paris. As with the Thane of Cawdor, it appears that evil also has its legitimacy and its *de jure* succession.

The account of the War of the Roses is full of the kind of imagery that Shakespeare uses for the disintegration of social order. The destructive energy of storm and tempest is prominent, and so are the meteors, comets, and "exhalations" that represent social disorder. We also have the prophecies,

oracles, soothsayings, and rumours that accompany the viola-
tion of time, when the sense of the present is dislocated into a
"hideous dream" of the future, "When avoided grace makes
destiny." The uncanny "clock" passages in *Richard III* have the
same sense of the "untimely." From the second part of
Henry VI on, the action is polarized around a good and a bad
Gloucester, like much of the action of *King Lear*, and with
Richard III the cycles of fortune and history stop turning for
an instant and show us an apocalyptic separation of order and
chaos, the human and the demonic. Richard III, in becoming
himself alone, also becomes the circumference of a shadow-
world of murdered ghosts who return on All Souls' Day to
carry him off. When he says:

> By the apostle Paul, shadows to-night
> Have struck more terror to the soul of Richard
> Than can the substance of ten thousand soldiers
> Armed in proof, and led by shallow Richmond

he completes the theme of shadow and substance that began
with Talbot, Talbot being the murdered "primal father" of
this group of plays.

The isolated characters at the other pole are isolated through
consciousness. They become aware of what is happening, and
speak for us because in that moment of awareness they join
the audience, and see the action around them as a spectacle.
For a philosopher, isolation is the first act of consciousness.
I am myself alone, he says, and the rest of the world then
becomes objective to him. But for the hero of a tragic action,
isolating one's mind in this way is deeply terrifying. In the
tragic society one's life is in one's function or relation to

others, and when the group preserves one's real life, isolation becomes a confronting of nothingness. Cowards and traitors are isolated: the consciousness, once withdrawn from its social context, discovers that doubts are traitors and that conscience makes cowards. With Timon, it "Walks, like contempt, alone."

An example of the paradoxical isolating of consciousness in a tragic action is this speech of Henry IV:

> O God! that one might read the book of fate,
> And see the revolution of the times
> Make mountains level, and the continent,
> Weary of solid firmness, melt itself
> Into the sea! and, other times, to see
> The beachy girdle of the ocean
> Too wide for Neptune's hips; how chance's mocks
> And changes fill the cup of alteration
> With divers liquors: O, if this were seen,
> The happiest youth, viewing his progress through,
> What perils past, what crosses to ensue,
> Would shut the book, and sit him down and die.

Henry IV is one of Shakespeare's successful heroes, turning the wheel of history one stage at a time, his perspective a short-range practical one, his attention clearly focussed on what he is doing. It is significant that for such a man a moment of enlarged consciousness should also be a moment of depression. Suddenly he sees, in the framework of this gloomy Ovidian cosmology, a vision of the wheel of history turning forever, and himself in the Sisyphus role that we have spoken of in connexion with the ruler. As soon as his mind gets sufficiently detached from his situation to get a properly philosophical view of it, the first question that occurs to him is simply, why go on with it? We should think of Sisyphus as a happy man, according to Camus. Henry is not a happy man: he is a bothered man, with insomnia and a nagging conscience; but if he were a philosopher-king he would give up entirely. The limiting of his consciousness to his specifically royal function is all that keeps him going.

When one's real life is in one's loyalties and actions, all that the isolated mind can attain is an awareness of absurdity. Life is an idiot's tale, signifying nothing; the question is whether to be or not to be; the gods kill us for their sport. These famous utterances are not merely expressions of despair; they are the only kind of philosophical reflexion that we are likely to get from a tragedy, unless it is a philosophical tragedy in the tradition of Seneca, like Fulke Greville's *Mustapha*, and not many such tragedies belong in the public theatre. Life is real and life is earnest only as long as we do not try to disentangle reality from illusion, earnestness from play. Once withdrawn from the course of action that holds us within our society, chaos is come again.

Some of the rebel-figures have a certain temperamental affinity for isolation. Brutus, and, in a different way, Cassius, have something of a philosophical temperament, which means that they are likely to be overthrown in the world of action and yet achieve a different kind of triumph through the fortitude of consciousness. Brutus says: "I shall have glory by this losing day," and with him a victory of the mind is neither cheap nor entirely hollow. Macbeth, somewhat unexpectedly, also turns out to be his own best commentator, in contrast to his wife's more common procedure of thrusting the sense of guilt into the unconscious. If Othello, as Eliot says, is cheering himself up in his final speech, Macbeth is certainly cheering himself down in his soliloquies, painting a picture of soul-sickness with the greatest accuracy of detail. Hamlet's contemplative temperament, keeping him to a "discourse of reason" which interferes with his spontaneity of action, makes him one of a group of melancholy characters involuntarily hooked in to a tragic action for which they have little liking or affinity. Bosola, Bussy, and Vendice are other examples. Hamlet, in particular, sees things, not objectively, but as the objectified counterpart of a withdrawn and melancholy disposition, in short a nauseated vision.

But often a character is isolated from the action without any mental resources for isolation. Coriolanus, for example, is a most unreflective hero: we noticed how as soon as he is exiled from Rome he joins the Volscians without any apparent twinge of conscience. The simplest and starkest account of the isolating of an unreflective temperament, however, is *Othello*. Othello is attached to the society of the Venetian Senate as a capable and trusted public servant, but at the centre of the Senate sits the spiteful old pantaloon Brabantio, with the voice of the accuser, pointing to the one thing that isolates Othello, his black body, and insisting on the "unnatural" quality of Desdemona's love for him. This is the foundation on which Iago builds, Iago having only to make Othello's mind black too. He is helped in doing this, partly by the fact that jealousy in itself tends to create an enclosed prison-world, and partly by a curious quality in Othello's imagination that can only be called cosmological. Othello woos Desdemona by creating for her amusement an entire world of marvels and adventures: it may have been all true, but it is clear that its effect on Desdemona did not depend on its truth. Within this world of romance, love gives form and embodiment to a social function. Under Iago's influence Othello takes the initiative in creating a hell of "goats and monkeys," where the voice in his ear is a demonic parody of a creative word. In one of those apparently pointless remarks by which Shakespeare indicates the shape and direction of his imagery, Emilia alludes to this creation of a private universe. Desdemona says she would not be unfaithful "for the whole world," and Emilia says that in that case "having the world for your labour, 'tis a wrong in your own world, and you might quickly make it right." When Othello has put out the last light in his black world, he sees, over against it, "another world," a perfect chrysolite or rejected pearl in which Desdemona's love and chastity insensibly modulate into the memory of his services to the state, just as his first awakening of jealousy brought with it a sense that "Othello's occupation's gone."

At the beginning of *King Lear*, we see the hero preparing to take the fatal step of depriving himself of his own social context. He will exchange the reality for the "name" of king, and instead of being loved by his subjects for his qualities, he will be loved by his daughters for himself alone. All seems to go well until, with Cordelia's "nothing," he finds himself staring into the blankness of an empty world. Those who love Lear love him according to their bond, the tie of loyalty which is their own real life. Who is Lear to be loved apart from that? That is, what is the identity of a king who is no longer a king? Lear starts asking questions about his own identity very early, and he gets a variety of answers. "My lady's father," says Oswald; "Lear's shadow," says the Fool, a much shrewder person than Oswald. The word "shadow" recalls Richard II, seeking his identity in a looking-glass. The substance of Lear and of Richard is royalty and loyalty: their shadows, or spectres as Blake would call them, are the subjective Lear and Richard confronting an objective world which is unreal because they are. They are in the position of the Biblical Preacher who was once king in Jerusalem, and who now knows only that all is "vanity," that is, vapour, mist, shadow. Or, to put the essential paradox more clearly, all things are full of emptiness.

At the beginning of *King Lear* we are introduced to Edmund, making polite murmurs about his duty and services, and immediately after the abdication scene Edmund appears again, saying,

> Thou, Nature, art my goddess: to thy law
> My services are bound.

One of the first points made about Edmund is his contempt for astrology. This contempt has nothing to do with anybody's belief in astrology, but is purely a matter of consistent imagery. The royalty of Lear held his society bound to that greater nature which is symbolized by the stars in their courses, the world of order and reason that is specifically the world of human nature. With the abdication we are now wholly confined to the lower physical nature of the elements, an amoral world where the strong prey on the weak. It is this lower nature, the Dionysian wheel of physical energy and fortune, to which Edmund attaches himself. He is Gloucester's "natural" son, and on that level of nature he will act naturally.

In this situation Lear is joined by the Fool and Kent, Kent being also a fool, as the Fool himself informs him, for we are now in a world where it is folly to be genuinely loyal. The Fool is a "natural" in the sense of representing something still unspoiled and innocent in the middle of a fallen nature. The usual symbol of this natural innocence is the child, the two being associated in the proverb "children and fools tell the truth." Nothing shows the royal nature of Lear more clearly than his tenderness for his "boy"; this tenderness becomes increasingly parental, and the great cry at the end, "And my poor fool is hanged!", represents a blending together in his mind of the two people he loves as a father. Goneril habitually refers to her husband as a fool because he is a "moral fool," full of childish scruples he ought to outgrow. Goneril, of course, does not distinguish the childish from the childlike, and so does not believe that the Fool really is a fool, as she cannot understand innocence. The jokes of the Fool, like those of the clowns in *Hamlet*, consist largely of puns, conundrums, and parodies of syllogisms, and so establish a comic counterpart to the tragic action in which absurdity is made convincing.

The philosopher first isolates himself and then stabilizes himself: he remains a sane, conscious, normal intelligence, and nature therefore appears to him as an order, though a relatively static order or chain of being, not the controlled force that it is to the successful ruler. In the tragic vision whatever isolates the hero pushes him much further than this, into the nausea of Hamlet or the hell-worlds of Othello and Macbeth. Lear is pushed directly toward the *hysterica passio* he so dreads, and nature therefore appears to him in the objective form of madness, which is storm and tempest. On the heath, a mad shadow confronts a mad shadow-world, for the storm is described in a way that makes it not simply a storm but chaos come again, the cracking of nature's moulds. The turning point of the scene is Lear's prayer, a prayer which addresses no deity, but the dispossessed of the earth. In this prayer Lear finds his human identity again, though in a very different context from kingship, and immediately after it Poor Tom appears.

No one can study *King Lear* without wondering why Edgar puts on this Poor Tom act for Lear's benefit. He has to go into disguise, of course, but none of Cornwall's spies are likely to be listening, and elsewhere on the heath open conspiracy is discussed under the storm's cover. Just as, in a comic context, Petruchio shows Katherina the reflection of her own shrewishness in himself, so Poor Tom is the providence or guardian spirit that shows Lear the end of his journey to find his own nature. What is the nature of man? There are many answers, but Lear is now in an order of nature so disordered that Edmund is called a "loyal and natural boy." The Fool, who really is a loyal and natural boy, is all that is left of the "desperate train" which Regan pretends to be afraid of. The question then takes the form: what is left of a man when we eliminate his social and civilized context and think of him purely as an object in physical nature? The answer given by satire is the Yahoo, the natural man with his natural vices, of which Gulliver's greater cleanliness and intelligence are merely sophistications. The softer and gentler answer given by comedy is Caliban, nature without nurture, the deformed slave who is loyal to the wrong master and resentful of the right one. The answer given by tragedy is

Poor Tom, that eats the swimming frog, the toad, the tadpole, the wall-newt and the water; that in the fury of his heart, when the foul fiend rages, eats cow-dung for sallets; swallows the old rat and the ditch-dog; drinks the green mantle of the standing pool; who is whipped from tithing to tithing, and stock-punished, and imprisoned.

The imagery is deliberately nauseating, and we notice again that nausea is deeply involved in man's contemplation of himself in a physical context. "Is man no more than this?" asks Lear wonderingly, but he has had his answer. "Thou art the thing itself," he says, and starts tearing at his clothes to remove what is left of his relation to human society. Poor Tom, a better mirror of identity than Richard had, is trying to stand between Lear in front of him and the abyss of non-being inhabited by the foul fiends behind him, and provide, so to speak, a solid bottom for Lear's fall into nature. If Lear had been granted the few moments of rest he so needed, Edgar's efforts might have preserved his sanity.

Besides the intricate series of puns on "natural" in *King Lear*, there is also an emphatic repetition of the words "all" and "nothing." In giving away his crown, Lear gave "all" to his daughters, and, as the Fool keeps insisting, he is now "nothing." Richard II uses the same words:

> Make me, that nothing have, with nothing grieved,
> And thou with all pleased, that hast all achieved!

The word "nothing" has two meanings: it is a grammatical negative meaning "not anything," and it is a positive noun meaning "something called nothing." Poetry has been exploiting the puns involved in this double meaning ever since

Polyphemus in the Odyssey screamed that "nobody" was blinding him. In Shakespeare the word nothing, when it means something called nothing, usually refers to the loss of essence, not to the end of existence. "Edgar I nothing am," says Edgar, meaning that he ceases to be Edgar though he goes on living; "the king is a thing of nothing," says Hamlet, meaning that Claudius is not really the king although he is on the throne; Timon says his friends "are to me nothing," meaning that friends have vanished from his life although life goes on for both. Timon says later "nothing brings me all things," referring to his approaching death, but there he is emphasizing a nihilism in it which is symbolized by his suicide. Goneril and Regan, however brusque and insensitive, show a certain hard common sense in their attitude to Lear, and are not revealed as evil until they separate him from what is left of his society. The outcry made about their cruelty in cutting off his "train" seems excessive at first, but is deeply rooted in the convention of the play. That act shows that they do not merely "seek his death"; they seek rather his annihilation. To murder Lear, and thereby get the noisy old nuisance out of the way, would show less real malice than wiping out the society he commands and letting him go on living. The latter obliterates the idea or real form of Lear, so to speak: it strikes at a deeper life than his physical one.

We have spoken of the type of rhetoric in Shakespeare which, as in Ulysses' speech on degree, Canterbury's beehive figure, or Menenius' fable of the belly and members, sets out a conservative view of society and sees it as a structure of natural order. To see it in this way, the appearance or façade of society must be regarded as also the reality of society. This is life seen from the point of view of action, where reality and appearance are the same thing. The rhetoric of isolation, as we find it particularly in the fourth acts of *King Lear* and *Timon of Athens*, is mainly a bitter denunciation of human hypocrisy, the contrast of reality and appearance. Lear and Timon are in a position to see this hypocrisy because, like the hypocrite, they have separated their real selves from their social relationships. The denunciation has the oracular ring of truth, but of a truth that we cannot do anything about. It is the voice, not of pure detachment, but of a detached consciousness. The feelings are still engaged: Timon is still an outraged idealist and Lear a helpless king. We feel that both Timon and Lear are "unreasonable," that the workings of the sexual instinct in a "simpering dame" hardly call for so much horror, that ingratitude could be shrugged off as well as screamed at. Eliot takes a similar view of the excessive disgust in Hamlet's view of his mother's re-marriage. But in the tragic vision, where one starts with a social order in which reality *is* appearance, the discovery of sin and hypocrisy and corruption cannot be made by the reason, but only by *saeva indignatio.*

Lear has turned his world inside out by his abdication: the order of nature becomes first the disorder of the heath, for an impotent king creates a waste land, and then the perverted order of the Cornwall society, descending through chaos to hell. The first shade encountered in Dante's hell is a Pope who did not want to be a Pope: "Che fece per viltà il gran rifiuto." The "gran rifiuto," the voluntary surrender of one's appointed function, is a frequent source of tragedy in Shakespeare, though it is never made from "viltà," but for heroic reasons. It is clear that Titus Andronicus could have been Emperor of Rome if he had wanted to be: by withdrawing in favour of the weak and vicious Saturninus he allows a perverted social order to be set up, in which he is reduced to the impotence of shooting protests attached to arrows into the Emperor's garden. The withdrawal creates two concentric spheres of tragic action, so to speak, which might be described as the Goths within and the Goths without. The central action is the mutual revenge of Tamora and Titus, grotesque and horrible to the verge of absurdity—or perhaps not merely to the verge, as it seems to me that absurdity is one of the central dramatic points of the play. This action is contained by a peripheral one in which Titus' son Lucius, like Coriolanus (to whom he is compared in the dialogue), though more successfully, returns with an alien army and destroys the malefactors. This action is the morally intelligible action of the tragedy of order, ending in a post-tragic contract which restores the pre-tragic one.

In *King Lear* and *Timon of Athens* there are also two concentric spheres of action, but their relation is reversed: here the morally intelligible action is inside and the absurd one contains it. The society that Timon attempts to create by his prodigal generosity is the typically Athenian society of the symposium, the festivity of wine and reason which is in Plato the embodiment of the idea of society. The word embodiment is not strictly Platonic; it suggests rather incarnation, and incarnation suggests the symposium of Christ in which two things are important: the betrayal of Christ and the communion with him. The fact that Timon's guests are devouring his substance, in other words eating him, and repeated phrases about "tasting" his bounty, apply communion imagery to him by way of parody. The Biblical echoes of the fact that his guests are traitors come in to some phrases of Apemantus:

"It grieves me to see so many dip their meat in one man's blood—the fellow that sits next him now, parts bread with him, pledges the breath of him in a divided draught, is the readiest man to kill him."

The same senators (probably) who cut so poor a figure in relation to Timon are also those who uphold the law against Alcibiades' plea for pardoning a hot-blooded homicide. Their argument is the same as that of the Prince of Verona: "Mercy but murders, pardoning those that kill," but the context is different. Alcibiades is pure hero, a soldier whose life is dedicated to the risk of death, and, with his unfailing courtesy to Timon, he stands out as a character who, if not attractive, is at any rate not contemptible. In Plutarch's scheme of "parallel lives" Alcibiades is the Greek counterpart of Coriolanus, and Plutarch remarks, in comparing the two, that Coriolanus with all his virtues could not make himself loved, and Alcibiades with all his vices could not make himself hated. Shakespeare could not have read Plutarch's account and missed the point that Alcibiades was a scoundrel, but he has other dramatic uses for him. Alcibiades, with his drum and his two whores, is the kind of rebel-figure who always gets control of a society if there is no order-figure. He will, as he says:

> Make war breed peace, make peace stint war, make each
> Prescribe to other as each other's leech.

That is, he will pull Athens back on the wheel of fortune where the main energies of life are expressed in war rather than peace.

Timon had a different conception of society, and, wrongheaded as his attempts to achieve it may have been, one feels that he is rightly called "noble." In his exile he has acquired something of the more realistic view of human nature that the order-figure has, a view which has a lower opinion of generosity and a higher one of death. He is asked to take command of Athens against Alcibiades, and at this point he makes his "gran rifiuto." Like Lear, he is not easily convinced of the moral indifference of nature: nature sustains him with roots and water, but he hopes, and half expects, that it will destroy everybody else. But Athens refuses to be destroyed: it makes a deal with Alcibiades and the wheel of history goes on turning.

Thus the inner action of the play is a very ironic tragedy of order, in which a peaceful but inglorious society expels a military leader, only to have him return and compel it to revert to the ordinary cycle of life. The containing action— I call it that because, although the play concludes with Alcibiades beating his drum, Timon is the hero, and his is the action we remember afterwards—is the total isolation of Timon from his society. This action is like a parody of, for instance, Aristophanes' *Acharnians*, where the good citizen (Dicaeopolis) withdraws from the war of Athens and Sparta and celebrates his own feast of Dionysus at home, driving away all the parasites and politicians who come to interfere with him. In *Timon of Athens* the peaceful festival and the beating off of interference belong to totally opposed conditions. The symposium is a social ideal of which human nature, in the tragic vision, is not capable; Timon's life in exile is a fierce and lonely pastoral, and the pastoral, whether attempted by a society of shepherds or by a solitary noble savage, is also not a possible way of life in a tragic context. We have suggestions of this in Shakespeare as early as the pastoral speech of Henry VI, already referred to.

Like Lear on the heath, Timon cannot remain in the philosopher's position: that can only be done by someone in the midst of society, like Apemantus. Apemantus is a cynic (hence the repetition of "dog" in connection with him), with Stoic ideals of invulnerability, and as such he is not "opposite to humanity," as one of Timon's guests complacently says, but he is constantly aware of what humanity is. Timon in exile, trying to be opposite to humanity, tries also to ally himself with everything destructive in nature. His sense of outrage and his isolation prevent him both from exploiting human nature like Alcibiades and from a consistent vision of absurdity, such as Apemantus has. The only end for him is suicide, and he dies "Upon the beached verge of the salt flood," the sea representing chaos as the storm does in *King Lear*. The story of Timon, as a tragedy, is absurd, in the existential and not the moral sense, and so the vision of absurdity contains and enfolds the vision of the turning wheel of fortune.

In *King Lear* there is also an inner and an outer action. The inner action is a straight tragedy of order, with Gloucester the martyred father, Edmund the rebel-figure, and Edgar the nemesis. Its general context is that of the original sin in which the killing of the father becomes a central symbol of guilt: as Gloucester says in an ironic anticipation of his own betrayal:

> Our flesh, my lord, is grown so vile
> That it doth hate what gets it.

Gloucester's is a morally intelligible tragedy, passing, like the story of Oedipus, through a terrifying blinding and ending, again like Oedipus, in comparative serenity. Gloucester is physically isolated from the action, and, unlike Lear, he tries to make an end of himself physically, by suicide. Edgar appears to him in various disguises, as he does to Lear, and with the same object of guiding him past the abyss of non-being. Everything can be explained in Gloucester's tragedy: he had a moral flaw that made him gullible, and he had a proud mind, shown in his boast about the sexual exploit that produced Edmund. At the moment when Edgar's nemesis is completed, Edgar says:

> The gods are just, and of our pleasant vices
> Make instruments to plague us;
> The dark and vicious place where thee he got
> Cost him his eyes.

For all his courage and devotion Edgar never seems to be able to resist remarks like this, and even as a comment on Gloucester it seems a trifle facile. It is always possible to say that if the hero had acted otherwise (in most cases, more virtuously) the tragedy would not have occurred. The point of saying it about Gloucester is apparently to emphasize the sense of his tragedy as fitting into a moral order.

But the fact that Gloucester's tragedy is morally explicable goes along with the fact that Gloucester is not the main character of the play. If we apply such formulas to Lear they give us very little comfort. What does the good sport at Edmund's making prove when we have Goneril and Regan "got 'tween lawful sheets?" At the blinding of Gloucester, Cornwall is fatally wounded by a servant. This is again part of the moral sense that Gloucester's tragedy makes, Edgar's axiom "Ripeness is all" being closely related to the view of Job's comforters that a full and completed life is the natural result of virtue. Gloucester appeals for help on this basis,

"He that will think to live till he be old" being an ironic anticipation of his later desire to cut his own life short. Another servant remarks of Regan:

> If she live long
> And in the end meet the old course of death,
> Women will all turn monsters.

Well, it is true that Regan is poisoned, but Cordelia is hanged. Regan's death proves nothing, except perhaps the reality of nothingness.

King Lear has been called a purgatorial tragedy, and if that means a structure even remotely like Dante's *Purgatorio*, we should expect to see, as we see in Dante, existence being taken over and shaped by a moral force. Our understanding of the tragedy, then, would have that qualified response in it that is inseparable from a moral or conceptual outlook. It is true that Lear has suffered terribly, but he has thereby gained, etc. Suffering is inevitable in the nature of things, yet, etc. But, of course, Lear is not saying anything like this at the end of the play: what he is saying is that Cordelia is gone, and will never, never come back to him. Perhaps he thinks that she is coming back to life again, and dies of an unbearable joy. But we do not see this: all we see is an old man dying of an unbearable pain. The hideous wrench of agony which the death of Cordelia gives to the play is too much a part of the play even to be explained as inexplicable. And whatever else may be true, the vision of absurd anguish in which the play ends certainly is true.

We began this discussion by establishing a distinction between authentic tragedy and melodrama. By melodrama I

mean a dramatic vision that confirms the audience's stock
moral responses: that achieves comedy primarily by applaud-
ing the hero and tragedy primarily by punishing the villain.
Such a dramatic vision is aesthetic in the perverted Kierke-
gaardian sense of externalizing man's ethical freedom. In a
sense it is anti-tragic, providing as it does a justification for
a tragic action that comes from something outside tragedy,
and so, really, explaining tragedy away. In authentic tragedy
what we see as external to us is, first of all, the order of nature,
with its servomechanism the wheel of fortune. Nature and
fortune, when seen from the point of view of the human
situation, constitute a vision of absurdity and anguish, what
design is in them being unintelligible to human imagination,
human emotions, and ultimately to human moral instincts.
Introducing thunder as the voice of disapproving divinity in
Tourneur is melodramatic, in the sense that it presents God
as confirming the moral prejudices that the audience already
has. The thunder in *King Lear* is the tragically authentic
voice of nature crumbling into chaos, though Lear himself
half hopes that it is making a comment on his situation. The
gods in Greek tragedy are not melodramatic, because they
are, as Elizabethan critics saw, assimilable with nature; they
emphasize the morally unintelligible aspect of human anguish
instead of neutralizing it. Seneca is not as melodramatic as
his influence would suggest, but his deep Stoic belief in a
morally intelligible natural order gives his tragedies a potenti-
ally melodramatic quality which accounts for a good deal of
that influence.

It is perhaps on this basis that we can come to terms with
the venerable puzzle: is tragedy compatible with a Christian

view of life? Christianity as an institutional religion, **giving**
a mysterious sanction to society's moral anxieties, is inconsis-
tent with tragedy because it is simply incapable of the tragic
vision. But the reality, that is, the myth, of Christianity is
very different: it tells us that all we can see, out there, of the
activity of God in human life comes to a focus in the absurd
and anguished figure of the crucified Christ. The heroic effort
which Christ made against the irony of universal death was,
Christianity tells us, successful. But the earthly end of his
career, so far as we can see it, was exactly the same as the end
of a failure, and of all Christian doctrines, the doctrine that
Christ died is the most difficult to disbelieve. The moral or
melodramatic attitude can do nothing with this crucifixion
vision except reverse it, seeing it as followed by a second moral
judgment in which Christ is the judge and those who condemn him are his writhing victims. In this double gyre of
sado-masochism there is no place for the heroic struggle against
irony which is, so to speak, the tragic enzyme. A genuinely
tragic Christian attitude would see suffering as a participation
in the passion of a hero who was both divine and human, and
so would establish a place within Christianity for the tragic
hero.

I use the religious example only as an analogy to the tragic
structure in Shakespeare. If there is anything more than
absurdity and anguish in the death of Lear or Othello, it
comes, not from anything additional that we can see in or
know about the situation, but from what we have participated
in with them up to that moment. When Macbeth sees life
as a meaningless idiot's tale, we can see that such a vision of
absurdity is right for Macbeth at that point, and is therefore

true for him. But it is not the whole truth, even for him, because he is capable of articulating it, nor for us, because we have shared with him, however reluctantly, an experience too broad and varied to be identified with its inevitable end, however desired an end. Tragedy finds its ultimate meaning neither in heroic death nor in ironic survival, nor in any doctrine deducible from either, but in its own re-enactment as experience. It was his perception of this element in tragedy that led Nietzsche to his conception of assenting to a recurrent experience as the mark of the hero, but that takes us up a blind alley. The hero of a tragedy ultimately includes the audience who form the *substance* of the hero, like Talbot's soldiers, who participate in a ritual act of suffering in which the suffering is not real but the awareness of it is. The awareness survives the play and gives it a death-and-resurrection pattern which is expressed by Keats in his sonnet on reading *King Lear*:

> Let me not wander in a barren dream,
> But when I am consumed in the fire,
> Give me new Phoenix wings to fly at my desire.

In the tragedy of isolation the hero becomes a scapegoat, a person excluded from his society and thereby left to face the full weight of absurdity and anguish that isolated man feels in nature. He is thus dramatically in the position of the villain of melodrama, but the feeling of moral separation of the bad character from the good (or at any rate not so bad) audience is not there. Or if it is there, it does not have the same relevance. The dreadful pact consummated by Iago with the words "I am your own for ever" has bound us too, and we feel no deliverance from Iago's prospective death, because he is one of the dark powers who have also humiliated us. In a tragic story there are plausible reasons why a character gets into a scapegoat position, but they are never so plausible as to make the response "of course I should never have done that" relevant. Whatever the tragic hero has done, we are never so wise or virtuous that we cannot participate in the consequences of his fall with him. At the end of a comedy a new society is created or restored and the characters go off to a new life out of our reach. Even those who exclude themselves from this society, like Jaques in *As You Like It* or Marchbanks in *Candida*, have secrets in their hearts we can only guess at. At the end of a tragedy, where most of the main characters are usually dead in any case, there is a far greater sense of mystery, because (paradoxically) it is not what the characters have learned from their tragic experience, but what we have learned from participating in it, that directly confronts us.

We read in Frazer of an ancient ritual (how much it was ever practised could hardly matter less) in which a divine king is killed at the height of his powers and ritually eaten. His body and blood pass into the bodies and blood of his eaters, and thereby create a single divine body out of them. Elizabethan tragedy was more primitive than Greek tragedy in bringing down the hero on the stage, in sight and almost within touch of most of the audience. But, whatever may be true of melodrama, tragedy does not unify the audience in a mystical communion of this kind: so far as the theatre can do this, it does it in comedy, where a new social order is created and the audience applauds to show its agreement that this is what it wants. Tragedy individualizes the audience, nowhere more intensely than in the tragedy of isolation. Man is a creator as an individual; as a member of a society or species, he is a creature. The end of a comedy leaves him creaturely, invited to join a party to celebrate the creation of a new society, from the further fortunes of which he is of course excluded by the ending of the play. The end of a tragedy leaves him alone in a waste and void chaos of experience with a world to remake out of it. It is partly because of this insistent challenge to the spectator's re-creative powers that the great tragedies are so endlessly fascinating to critics: merely to experience them seems to demand commentary as part of one's response.

To go further with this point would take us into a fourth area of tragedy, which in Shakespeare would be the romances, including *Henry VIII*, seen as tragedies, and as the fulfilment of his tragic vision. I have already written a book on the romances as the fulfilment of Shakespearean comedy, and do not wish to cover the same ground again, even from a different point of view. But is is obviously possible to see *The Tempest* as a tragedy of order in which the dethroned prince acts as his own nemesis in another world, building up in that world a natural society, though according to a conception of nature that rises clear of history and the wheel of fortune. We can see *Cymbeline* as a tragedy of passion in which the division of loyalties between Rome and Britain, along with the separation of Posthumus and Imogen, are overcome as soon as the fatal female influence of the Queen disappears. We can see *The Winter's Tale* as a tragedy of the isolation of consciousness caused by Leontes' jealousy

which, like Lear's abdication, creates a waste land that extends
from Sicilia into Bohemia and dissolves in a chaos of storm
and death and devouring monsters. Here the memory of
Hermione is cherished so intensely that it becomes a new
existence.

These plays are no longer tragic in any sense in which we
have been using that term in these lectures. Yet they represent
another possible dimension of tragedy, of which the Greek
archetype is *Alcestis*, or perhaps even the satyr-play, in which
death is contained by the action and the emphasis is thrown
on participation in a continuing movement, the pensive pulsa-
tion of Blake's Urthona. The audience does not directly participate, but it catches the rhythm of participation in the dance
and song and in the innumerable links of reconciliation and
renewed partnership in which these plays end. As I have
tried to show elsewhere, they seem to point toward a world
where the antithesis of spectator and spectacle, the subject
confronting the object, no longer exists. Here the antithesis
of tragedy and comedy is also overcome, and with it the
antithesis of creator and creature. The paradox of tragedy, the
vision of what is at once natural and absurd, is united to the
paradox of comedy, a vision of what is equally natural and
absurd in a different context. Here there is neither a chaos
to re-create nor a new community floating away into the land
of dreams, but, like the island of *The Tempest* which is
Mediterranean and yet so curiously American as well, an
old world that is a brave new world, an inheritance of which
we are at last the rightful possessors.